CW01509189

KINSHIP CARING

ABOUT THE AUTHOR

Dr Rachael King (BSc Hons, PGCE, MSc, Doc.Ed.Ch.Psychol) is an experienced HCPC registered Practitioner Psychologist, an Educational and Child Psychologist, with over two decades experience with children as a teacher, family worker, lecturer, researcher and consultant. Rachael has worked with Children in Care (CIC) and adoptive families throughout her work as an Educational and Child Psychologist in the local authority and private sectors. Her experience ranges from supporting families, to training, use of therapeutic approaches and a broad range of work in a range of educational settings and children's homes. Rachael worked in the US education system as an Academic Program Director of Psychology and Child Development in a multicultural college. She is a passionate advocate of promoting positive change through supporting every child whilst considering their story, and prioritising the importance of relationships and their strengths and needs.

KINSHIP CARING

A complete guide for families

and the

Kinship Family App

Dr Rachael King

worthpublishing.com

KINSHIP CARING

First published 2024 by Worth Publishing Ltd
worthpublishing.com

© Worth Publishing Ltd 2024

All rights reserved. No part of this publication may be reproduced, stored in a retrieval system or transmitted in any form, or by any means, electronic, mechanical, photocopying, recording or otherwise, without the prior permission of the publishers, nor be otherwise circulated without the publisher's consent in any form of binding or cover other than that in which it is published and without a similar condition being imposed on the subsequent purchaser.

Printed and bound in Great Britain by Grosvenor Group (Print Services) Limited, Loughton, Essex.

British Library Cataloguing in Publication Data
A catalogue record for this book is available from the British Library

ISBN 9781903269428

Cover and text design by Anna Dadswell

To Xyla and Lexy

for being you
and keeping me grounded
through the journey

Acknowledgements

I would like to thank the following, with much gratitude: Martin Wood and Andrea Perry at Worth Publishing for their ongoing support and cooperation, their compassion, thoughtfulness and forward thinking in prioritising the understanding and voice of children and young people through the support of the adults around them … and of course, for the opportunity to be involved in this project and making the process such a pleasure.

My friend, colleague and supervisor Dr. Kait Baxter, a great psychologist and great person. EPCAPP, a wonderful group of Educational Psychologists, thank you for sharing your collective knowledge and experience.

To all those adults who listen to children and really hear them - thank you!

Contents

cont. . . .

The numbers in the text in boxes [ ] refer to where that information has come from: you'll find those references on p. 67

An invitation ...

Each day I will try to ...

like myself and to reach out to others
keep my curiosity & interests alive
do activities I enjoy that move my mind & body
be kind & considerate, especially to those in need
wind down & re-live the high points of each day
... and not feel guilty if I don't succeed.

Dr Phil Hammond
drphilhammond.com

To access your FREE Kinship Family App using the QR code, follow the steps below:

→ Scan the **QR** code

→ Create a **CourseWeDo** account

→ Add the coupon code **kc4275** at the checkout to get it free and click **Enrol Now**

→ The **Kinship Family App** will now be added to your **CourseWeDo** account for you to log in and access on any internet enabled computer or device whenever you want.

To access your FREE Kinship Family App *without* scanning the QR code, follow the steps below:

→ Go to **coursewedo.com**

→ Select **Apps** on the Home Page

→ Select **Kinship Family App**

→ Click the **Purchase** button

→ Create a **CourseWeDo** account

→ Add the coupon code **kc4275** at the checkout to get it free and click **Enrol Now**

→ The **Kinship Family App** will now be added to your **CourseWeDo** account for you to log in and access on any internet enabled computer or device whenever you want.

Please contact info@coursewedo.com if you need any assistance.

Introduction

This book provides guidance and support for anyone who, for whatever reason, finds themselves becoming a full time Kinship Carer in a Kinship Family, sometimes called 'Family and Friends Carers' or 'Special Guardians'. The book also, uniquely, contains your access to the Kinship Family App, which you can use at home and with your child's school (*see opposite and* p. 52).

On behalf of children in care, and especially those in kinship care, the author and publisher wish to express our heartfelt gratitude for the wonderful loving care you and so many other relatives and families provide in your role as Kinship Carers to the children who need you most.

The book is divided into the three parts to provide you with help, guidance and reference. We sincerely hope the book and the App will be resources you can draw on to help you, your child or children, and the other family members involved around you, to thrive.

HOW AND WHY A CHILD MAY COME INTO YOUR CARE

As you may know, kinship care is care provided by members of a child's extended family or friend network when the child can no longer live with their parents.

Kinship care is the most common form of 'out of home' care [1] both internationally, and in the UK, and is full-time care, expected to last a significant period of time. Kinship care can become a permanent arrangement or can provide an opportunity for a situation and/or relationships to settle and repair so the child can return to their birth parents. In the UK, it's thought that at least 200,000 children [2] are cared for by a relative, friend or other person connected to them. So, whilst we recognise it may not feel like it at times, you are not alone.

We hope this book will help you to feel empowered in your new and very important role, and to know where to find support if and when you need it.

What kinship care offers:
- It provides your child with warm, loving relationships
- It provides stability and security
- It may reinforce continuity for your child in their family and community
- It reinforces your child's sense of identity and self-esteem
- It may allow links with your child's parents to be preserved

What challenges might you face?
- Helping your child settle into your home, and feel safe and secure
- Respecting and managing your child's behaviours and emotions
- Adapting to the change in your lifestyle
- Managing increased demands on your time - possibly less time for yourself
- Coping with an increase in financial responsibility
- Forming a bond/trusting relationship with your child in a new way
- Possibly some impact on your existing relationships
- Possibly some impact on wider family and friends
- Exploring and accepting your child's experiences and how they think and feel about what is happening
- Dealing with the response (or lack of response) from others.

Why have we created this guide?
In the UK, all parliamentary parties acknowledge that -

> '... Kinship care is widely unrecognised, underappreciated and
> often poorly supported ...'.
> Kinship Parliamentary Task Force (2020), p. 7 [3]

And you may feel the same way! So, we aim to help put that right - we recognise
the pressures on all concerned, and that's why we've created this guide. It's also
why we have devoted a lot of careful attention to positive relationships, since
they are the key to a settled life for the child you are caring for, for you and for
everyone involved.

A bit of background
Kinship care often arises from difficult and complex situations. These may
lead to a child being formally 'looked after' by the local authority, or, to family/
friends offering their support to look after a child when the child's parents cannot
(so that the child does not become formally looked after by the local authority).

- In the UK, most kinship placements are informally arranged
- However, there are more formal arrangements such as a Special
  Guardianship Order (SGO) or a Child Arrangement Order (CAO)
  (*referred to in* Part 3 *of this book*, p. 46)
- Informal kinship arrangements do not have to be reported to the local
  authority and the authority does not have to assess these placements.
  This can mean that it can be difficult to know what support is available and
  where to get it [4]
- The experience of being a Kinship Carer and the support offered will vary
  across different local authorities

SOCIAL WORKER INVOLVEMENT

Sometimes children may enter kinship care following court proceedings in a formal arrangement, when they may have been in the care system already. If the arrangement for kinship care is formal, and since the child has become looked after via a court process, it is very likely that both the child and the Carer will have a social worker who will remain involved to support the transition (from living with their birth parent(s) to living with the Kinship Carer).

Informal arrangements (where a family member voluntarily looks after the child by arrangement with the child's parent(s)), mean that the child does not become 'looked after' (in the official sense) and the parent(s) retain parental responsibility. In these circumstances, it is *unlikely* that a social worker will be involved. An exception to this would be if there have been concerns about the safety of the child: if a child protection plan is in place, or if the child has been classed as a 'child in need,' following an assessment by a social worker.

If a social worker was involved *before* kinship care started, or they were involved in the transition into kinship care, it is likely they will remain involved.

The involvement of a social worker for children in kinship care is complex, and keeps changing. It is less clear for informal kinship care arrangements than in the formal arrangements which led to a social worker being assigned. There is also some ambiguity when a Special Guardianship Order (SGO, *see* p. 46) is in place and the child is cared for by a relative: under these circumstances, the social worker may not remain involved.

If we do not have a Social Worker, will the child I'm caring for be missing out?
Every family situation is unique and how your child comes to live with you will be unique. Although a social worker can offer access to support routes in certain circumstances, there are many other ways to access support. The charity Kinship (kinship.org.uk) is a great starting point and so is linking with your child's school (*see* p. 54).

If you have concerns about the safety of your child, always reach out to your local authority Children's Services, however formal or informal your kinship care arrangement.

CHILD PROTECTION

Although we have included many ways that kinship care can be such a positive, protective and loving set-up, it's important that you are aware of how your local authority's Children's Services can be involved in keeping your child safe.

There are a number of ways they can support children and their families. There is variation from area to area, but they tend to follow the following structure:

- **Universal Provision** Most children will get their needs met through Universal Provision. These are services available to all children without referral or assessment. This covers services such as GPs, Children's Centres, health services, leisure centres and libraries.
- **Early Help** When a need within a family cannot be met through the universal provision, then Early Help can be given. This is voluntary and is intended to help families at the early stages of when they need support. It aims to make sure families get the right support when they need it to prevent a child coming to harm. It is preventative, so minor problems are less likely to become much bigger issues.
- **Child in Need** If a child is thought to need extra support or services to ensure they can 'achieve or maintain a reasonable standard of health or development' (Section 17 Children Act 1989), they will be classed as a 'child in need' (CIN). All children with a disability are classed as a CIN. If a child is thought to be a CIN then an assessment will be carried out by a social worker, and a plan written, which will be reviewed regularly. This plan will outline what support is required, which agencies will supply the support, what the child and family members agree to do, and what outcomes are expected.
- **Child protection** This is a formal process that occurs if a child is thought to be at risk of significant harm: the process will look different depending on the situation. A concern can be raised by anyone (as a 'referral') and has to be followed up by the local authorities Children's Services. There will often be a strategy discussion (meeting), enquiries and an assessment, an initial child protection conference and a child protection plan prepared. You can find out more at Child protection - Family Rights Group (frg.org.uk).

In this book, we'll be referring to 'your child', since, whilst you may not be the parent of the little person coming into your home (or the big one, if you are the Kinship Carer of a teenager), we believe that your relationship with them is what will make the most difference to their lives and happiness. Writing about 'the child' or 'the young person' is too impersonal! Your child and you are what matters most.

Throughout the guidance in this book, and on the Kinship Family App, we also recognise that the age of your child can be anything from that of a small baby to an older adolescent. So whenever a particular course of action is suggested, of course please vary it, according to the age of your child, your own way of doing things and what you both find useful and enjoyable.

PART I
Help and guidance during the initial transition into Kinship Care

Your child's arrival can often happen quickly in response to a crisis or emergency, which may mean you have very limited time to prepare. The transition for Kinship Carers from looking after themselves, to also looking after a child or children who may well be distressed when they arrive, presents many possible challenges, as everyone adjusts to the new situation and responsibilities.

Kinship Carers are rarely given advice or information about your rights before your child comes to live with you [1]. In fact 95% of Kinship Carers said they received no training to prepare them for the role [2].

Sometimes there may be a social worker involved, who can support you and your child to settle. If so, they may have carried out an assessment before your child came to you. Or, you may not have had any involvement from a social worker, particularly if the arrangement is informal.

Whatever the legal status of the care arrangement or the circumstances which mean that your child has come to live with you, there will be similarities in the experience and needs of the children [3] which we aim to address in this book.

EARLY DAYS

When your child first comes to live with you, there will be immediate considerations and adjustments needed to help your family cope with the initial impact of this big transition for you both. In amongst whatever stresses have created the circumstances under which your child needs to come to live with you, there is the obvious issue that you are not their parent; you may have a different parenting style to the one your child is used to. You may be used to parenting a different generation, so it can be important to update your style a bit! - as you start this new chapter of your lives together.

It's also possible that your child's experience of being parented may have been repeatedly disrupted in some way. When this happens, your children may have had their 'stress response' activated, which can lead to what's known as 'toxic stress': in other words, a level of stress which a child can't manage alone. This may mean they stay at a high stress level, tense, on edge, possibly reactive, even when the situation around them has improved, for example when they come to live with you.

To restore your child's stress response to where it should be, and helping them feel safe, relaxed and happy, they need to experience warm relationships with caring, responsive adults [4] - and that means you! Having nurturing and loving relationships with you as their Kinship Carer and others amongst your family members will be the crucial foundation to helping your child recover from any traumatic experiences they have encountered [5], and for their future development.

First steps

The first steps towards your child beginning to settle and feel a sense of belonging in their new home will be practical in nature: for example, preparing their bedroom so they have a space in your home that is 'their own', which they can personalise, and where they can begin to feel a sense of safety and retreat to, if they get overwhelmed. Show them where everything is in your home, where they can put their things, any routines you have already as a family, spaces they can play and do homework, how to get a drink/snack and so on.

For older children and teenagers to feel this is a home where they can have a sense of belonging, it's important that they have some independence and can feel they can have a shower/get a snack when they need or want to.   They may not take all of this in at once, so you may have to be flexible: a 'little and often' approach and revisiting all the new things in a fun and laid-back way will make all this less daunting. When there is toxic stress around for any of us, our memory can be affected, so expect to need to say things more than once. And that's OK - they'll remember more once they start feeling safer.

In these very first hours, days and months, it may help you to look for opportunities to do little, kind and thoughtful things, a key to building your relationship in this new way. So, for example, making their favourite meal, going for an ice cream together, popping a nice note in their pocket to find later, having a popcorn and movie night on the sofa together. For older children and teens it will be important that you join them in their interests - so they get a sense of 'being with' (which may take you well out of your comfort zone!). Join them in learning a dance or doing a joint challenge on TikTok, or ask if you can join them watching a football match. Make sure little gestures like this are not a 'reward' for, or conditional on, 'good behaviour', but instead, something which happens naturally as part of your new family life.

Your child may play or act like a child younger than their chronological age: this may be because they missed out on opportunities when they were smaller, or it may be that being away from and missing their familiar life, however challenging it was, means they may have gone backwards a bit for the moment, regressed. They may also feel very tired! - with so much change.

It's important to accept this, and not to miss these stages and move on developmentally before your child is ready, or expect too much too soon. It's OK for them to play and behave as a younger child would, and for you to respond as you would to a younger child. They will move on developmentally when they are ready and feel safe to do so (if this doesn't happen after a while, it would be important to find some professional support and guidance).

Missing familiarity and feeling sad

Although the life your child is coming to you from may have had its challenges and complications, there may be aspects they will miss, and a lot of familiarity will be lost. Their old home, their room and bed, the smells, the colours, the view, the journey home from school, their neighbours, maybe pets or a nearby park, or even a whole location, teachers and school friends - in addition of course to the person or people they are no longer living with. Where possible, it will be especially important to maintain or repair the relationship between your child and their birth parents (*see* Contact, p. 20). Accepting your child's sadness, or resistance to trying new things, as natural and understandable, will be important: we all need to time to make adjustments, and your child is going through a huge one.

On the other hand, your child may have things they really like to do or are interested in, so encourage and ensure they can continue with these. The familiarity, routines and enjoyment will encourage their sense of safety and help them develop a sense of belonging with you and realising they can trust that their priorities, interests and needs are important to you. When possible, make sure your child can continue with established clubs or groups, or support their plans to meet with friends. Connection with friends is important throughout childhood, but particularly during adolescence when your child's social support network will be a massive factor in their ability to cope with and process the changes in their life. This will also be key if your child does return to their birth parents: if they have maintained their friendships, it will also really help during further change and transition.

Further transitions

As your relationship with your child develops there will be further transitions - such as starting a new school, which may also be hard. It's yet more unfamiliarity, so expect tiredness, and perhaps a few setbacks as they acclimatise. Your child may benefit from having what are called 'transitional objects' which remind them of their previous life, or, an object which can remind them of you and help them remember that you are thinking about them. The object can also help them hold you in mind and feel connected, even when you are not physically together. This 'object' could be a small toy or soft animal for younger children, or even a small heart drawn on their hand. It could be a spray of your perfume or aftershave on their collar, or it could mean swapping keyrings with each other's photos in them [6].

It will be important that the choice of object is led and decided by your child - which toy, what small symbol would they like, in what colour pen, which photo? The choice may look very different for an older child or adolescent and may be more focused on technology - such as their phone, since this may be their connection to their birth parents, where that is possible, or friends. However, if they choose an object which might be more expected for a younger child, that's fine: the important thing is that whatever it is, the object holds meaning for your child.

Make sure that your child's school knows this object or symbol is important to your child, and so they can create a sensitive plan to allow it to be a part of your child's daily school life! It will be important for the transitional object to be a part of a well-managed, overall support plan for your child in school, with yourself, school and your child communicating openly and regularly (*see* p. 54 *for more information about the importance of your relationship with school*).

FEELING SAFE AND KEEPING SAFE

Often a child who comes into kinship care has faced challenges in their life. There may be very clear trauma which has occurred, either as a one-off event, or as part of an ongoing and complex situation. Your child will have had their own journey, which you will probably know something about (though not necessarily everything), and their foundations may be shaky. They may have had to build strong survival skills which will be embedded in their brain development. These survival skills may still show up when your child is with you too, even though the threats are no longer present - that's how our brains try to protect us. You know that your child is safe, but it may take a while for your child's brain to understand this deeply: so please be patient.

The good news is the young brain has 'plasticity' - it can create new pathways, so these survival skills won't always be needed. Over time, your 'parenting' can help create these new pathways, and what will help most will be your kind, loving and welcoming relationship with your child.

Your child will learn more from what you do than from what you say. Think about your own behaviour - we know that children notice everything! And they copy the adults around them - so be the 'model' for how you want your child to behave. Doing what you can to stay calm, warm, open and engaged (what is sometimes called 'regulated') will be very important. This will increase your child's feelings of safety (felt safety), because they'll experience you as a stable, calm and approachable person. And noticing how you manage your own feelings, especially during and after something upsetting or annoying, will also show/teach them how to stay calm or return to being calm, after upset. Life doesn't always make it easy for any of us to stay in that state! So please find the support you need so that you can remain open and relaxed as much of the time as possible.

Boundaries

What sorts of things enable children to feel secure? As well as giving them a consistent, warm and affectionate welcome, having clear and fair boundaries will also be an important part of your child feeling safe and developing a sense of trust. The boundaries you put in place should be simple, consistent, and with your child's safety in mind. Explain to your child why they are in place, listen to their views and allow some room for negotiation. This may be more challenging with older children and adolescents who are developing their own sense of autonomy, and even younger children who have had to learn to be self-sufficient to survive.

One of the things you'll also need to think about is around your child's use of technology, particularly during adolescence: think about when and how often you are on your own phone or device, and whether this matches the boundaries you have in place for your child.

If you're not familiar with how children and young people are using phones and devices at the moment, it'll be essential to find out, from your social worker (if you have one), your friends who know children of this age, or your child's school, about what is age appropriate. And, most importantly, safe, especially if there are constraints around contact with birth parents, for example.

It's also important to keep an open line of communication with your child about their use of their phone and other devices, and in particular social media, so that they see you as someone who is genuinely interested, non-judgmental and willing to engage in negotiation around something which for them might feel like a lifeline. There are features on phones which may be reassuring for you both, if you are in agreement about using them, such as being able to see each other's location, agreed times to text during the day, or sharing positive/upbeat photos or memes.

There may be times when your child wants to ask questions about something they come across online, and taking the approach we've just discussed means they will be more likely to come to you. It will be worth asking school about resources and advice around internet safety and ways to set up boundaries to keep your child safe online (and there are some in your Kinship Family App). Schools often set homework and have systems (dinner money, school trips, reports) which are online and they will be able to help you get set up. Local libraries may also have sessions you can access free of charge to help you develop your technology skills. The NSPCC has a specific section of resources for parents and carers of younger children to help keep them safe online nspcc.org.uk/keeping-children-safe/support-for-parents/techosaurus.

TELLING THE STORY OF COMING INTO KINSHIP CARE

At some point, your child will need to know their history and reasons for their new living arrangement with you, in order to develop a full sense of stability and permanence. They need a coherent story to understand the need for kinship care, so that they can come to feel that their life is better now than it was and that they are now safe, emotionally and physically, and they'll know what to say to friends.

As a Kinship Carer, it will be important for you to have an ongoing, open conversation with your child about their history, the reasons for their kinship care, as well as sharing current and future plans about living arrangements. This may mean answering their questions (insofar as you are able to) as non-judgmentally as possible, doing what you can to stay calm and loving if they get angry or upset with what you tell them.

Remember children are often extremely loyal to their birth parents, whatever has happened, and their memories may be different to what you tell them. Accept that they may have a different memory, or opinion, and empathise with their upset. Make sure you get some support for yourself from your friends or other adult family members, if you find this challenging, which would be entirely natural.

What's known as '*Life Story work*' is often recommended to help children make sense of their family history and why they are being looked after away from their birth parents [7]. If your child has a social worker they may be able to offer Life Story work or your local Educational Psychology Service may also be able to help (*see* p.60). There is a template you can use to start having discussions with your child about their past, present and future, as a 'Life Story book/journal' (kinship.scot/wp-content/uploads/2024/02/Life-Story-book.pdf) [8].

You may want to help your child create a memory box in your home to help them remember events which have happened in their life, and the people (and pets) who they may not see or not see as much. They can choose photos, trinkets, tickets or little notes you can write together or they can write privately. This can help them make sense of their memories and fill in some gaps. Maybe they can use a shoe box and decorate it how they like! [9] to keep somewhere private and safe.

UNDERSTANDING AND APPRECIATING EARLY EMOTIONS: YOUR CHILD'S AND YOUR OWN

Adversity and difficult times in a child's early life can impact their ability to be aware of and let adults know what they need and feel, and to stabilise their emotions. This may lead to children and young people communicating their unmet needs through unpredictable and sometimes difficult to manage behaviour, because they don't have the words or any other way to let us know what's happening for them. Understandably, a child who has had a hard start to life may have complex emotional and behavioural needs, especially related to expressing and managing their emotions, which may be all mixed up and painful [10].

Some behaviours you see at home when your child comes to live with you may be a communication of these unmet emotional needs and the 'big' emotions your child is experiencing as a result of their early experiences. Or sometimes, the feelings and behaviours may come out at school. It can be difficult to know how to deal with this, especially when the behaviour is confusing, loud, physical and sometimes scary. It may not seem like it, but those feelings and behaviours may scare your child as well! Your child may have emotional outbursts, seem 'shut down', not seem ready (or able) to show emotion, or try to control the behaviour of others.

It's possible that your child may have not had the opportunity in their early life to explore feelings and emotions with trusted and loving family members, and so not felt 'safe' to express how they feel. And that may have impacted their emotional development and ability to deal with stress or challenge, including the new ones they are encountering now that they have come to live with you in this not so familiar setting. Being sensitive to your child's emotions can help them develop the skills to manage their feelings, and be more comfortable with sharing with you what's going on inside them, and what they might need.

Finally, it's worth remembering that if your child has had a difficult start to life, they may not respond to traditional discipline or parenting approaches, which can be frustrating and leave you, their kinship carer, at a loss for what else to try. A distressed child will show less of these behaviours when they feel heard, when they feel safe and when the message they are trying to communicate is acknowledged.

That's unlikely to happen through an approach based on reward and punishment. But it can happen through focusing on the relationship between you and your child. Your child will often need your help to soothe themselves - they are not choosing to feel the distress, or to communicate this through their behaviour - so they need your support. You'll be able to help your child most effectively when you're feeling calm, accepting, empathic, and open to their range of emotions and experiences (*see also* Wellbeing, p. 50). Hard as it can be to not take things personally at times, it may be helpful to remember they are '*not doing it deliberately*' (the challenging behaviour): they are behaving as they are because they don't - *yet* - trust a better way to communicate their feelings and needs.

Prioritising relationship

The first step is to be curious about what might be triggering their behaviour, this is where your Kinship Family App can be very useful. It will help you think about what needs might be driving their behaviour, and then offer you lots of ideas for how to manage the situation, and to support your child, helping you find what works for you both.

Perhaps surprisingly, amongst other things, surprises, treats, special occasions (birthday/Christmas) can be very emotionally triggering for many children living in kinship care. This may be because they may feel that they are being disloyal to their birth parents, by taking part in celebrations and having fun, even though we know, as adults, that it's possible to have more than one feeling at once, sadness and joy. Or they may not feel they deserve nice things or treats, and they may feel guilty, without knowing why.

So, you may have planned a lovely treat or day out which ends up with your child becoming de-stabilised and showing some stress (a fight/flight response) which can be both confusing and perhaps hurtful, especially if you've made a special effort. Please try to stay curious and empathic. Try to imagine and feel the situation from your child's perspective. What could be underlying their reaction? Often small, low key treats and celebrations can feel safer for children in kinship care, and can encourage a more positive reaction. Over time, your child can learn that it is OK to do bigger nice things together, in a calm and planned way.

Your child's social and emotional skills may well be underdeveloped: through your relationship, you can provide opportunities for these to grow. Here are a some more ways you can do this.

Understanding and responding to emotions

- Show the emotions and behaviours you want to encourage in your child
- Develop ways to remain calm, even when you are experiencing strong emotional responses (p. 38-9)
- *Say* how you are feeling, rather than *showing* strong emotions through behaviour
- Model how to repair disagreements and show you are sorry (not just by saying it (p. 19))
- Accept and be responsive to your child's emotions and behaviours, to encourage trust to develop
- Use language thoughtfully (p. 33)
- Practice social situations your child finds difficult - use role play, or practise what they could say and do, to help them become more confident
- Share story books together to explore relationships and emotions
- Encourage your child to try new things, and new ways to use their strengths and skills
- Play games: model and practise turn-taking, ways to win and lose, share and negotiate - have fun whilst staying safe!
- If your child likes using devices, spend some screen time together - make it interactive, ask questions, take turns, let them lead
- When your child is upset, be curious, ask questions, have a guess and really listen to the reply. Be willing to be corrected if your guess is way off the mark. *Your willingness to have a go* will be the most important thing to them.

Importance of touch

Touch is an important part of development in children, close contact and touch can help develop relationships and trust. It helps children learn about their bodies, how touch feels, how it is received by other people (and animals), the different functions it can serve (e.g. calming and soothing, comfort and reassurance, expressing emotions such as empathy and care), and what kinds of touch are appropriate and what are not.

Unfortunately, some children's experiences can mean their interpretation of touch can be distorted or changed, especially if they have experienced inappropriate touch. There may be a need for them to develop a positive association with touch through experiencing appropriate touch and to learn the kinds of boundaries which you might expect they would already have learnt, but haven't been able to - yet. You will also have a preference for the touch you enjoy giving and receiving, and it will be a balancing act with your child to find a level of touch that eventually might work for you both, whilst holding in mind the benefits. It's important as the adult to be slow, respectful, gentle and cautious, and watch out for signs that things are getting too much for them or are unwelcome.

Depending on the age of your child it may be useful to have a direct conversation about acceptable boundaries and expectations, for them to know that both of you need to seek consent before there is physical touch and to see that you model this yourself.

Sadly, some children may have experienced abuse involving touch before they came to live in their kinship care family. Their need to re-establish boundaries and understand the importance of consent will be a priority, for them to feel safe and develop a trusting relationship with their carer. This can be tricky to address: if it is your situation, you may wish to get some external support to help. One useful resource for younger children is the NSPCC Pants programme *'Let's talk PANTS with Pantosaurus'* (*see* Useful Contacts p. 66) which helps children understand that their body belongs to them, and to tell a safe adult if anything makes them feel upset or worried.

Small ways to get used to positive touch

- ○ Soft, light touch on the back of the hand
- ○ Hand on arm/shoulder
- ○ Arm around shoulders
- ○ High five for positive accomplishment
- ○ Reassuring, gentle pat on the mid-back

Therapeutic Parenting

Therapeutic parenting is a nurturing parenting style with a focus on responding empathically. We can use this at any age, and the earlier the better. When our

---

KEY CONCEPTS OF THERAPEUTIC PARENTING INCLUDE:

- Strong routines
- Clear boundaries
- Predictability
- Advance warning - no surprises, however fun they might seem! Sudden change can be a signal for danger for your child, if they've experienced trauma previously
- Avoiding more traditional parenting techniques, such as 'time out' or rewarding good behaviour
- Having 'time in' instead of 'time out' when times get tough. Spend time with your child, interact, and gently help them become calm again (regulate) before working out together what needs to happen next
- Using natural rather than punitive consequences for distressed behaviour - this helps encourage linking cause and effect. For example, if they break their phone they won't have it to use until it's fixed or replaced, or if they stay up late, they will feel tired the next day
- Avoiding comments which might shame your child - your child's situation is not their fault. This could include not talking critically in your child's presence about the parent they are parted from

---

children trust that we are really trying to understand and take their feelings and wishes into account, through our empathy, it reduces their need to control the situation. The aim is to create a greater sense of harmony through expressing empathy, improving their social skills, helping them develop cause-and-effect thinking (*"If I do this then that will happen"*) and self-regulation (ability to soothe themselves, to become calm and relaxed again). It will also encourage the development of a strong bond between you and your child (secure attachment) and promotes their recovery from trauma.

You can find out more information on therapeutic parenting from the National Association of Therapeutic Parents (NAOTP) (*see* Useful Contacts, p. 66).

- Parent your child at the stage they are developmentally, not because of their age (see p. 9). Often children who have had to deal with difficult things may take a bit longer to reach milestones
- Acknowledge your child's internal experiences: for example, *"I'm wondering if you are feeling a bit muddly and upset by all these new things, is that how it is for you at the moment? That would be really understandable, if so"*
- Develop family ways of *showing sorry* rather than saying it - this may be too much for them just yet. For example, if your child breaks something, they could help tidy it up or fix it, rather than *saying sorry* or having their device taken off them. *"Sorry"* will come in time (like *"Please"* and *"Thank you"*) if they hear you saying these words, including to them, when appropriate
- Plan ahead. If your child is stealing food, have a box in the fridge of food he or she can take whenever they want. This removes the need for your child to try to stay in control by stealing. Also try having predictable meal and snack times, if you can, so they always know when and how they will get fed. Not knowing when you'll be fed can be a great source of anxiety for children, and food may also be a stand in for comfort when so much is unfamiliar

CONTACT: OPPORTUNITIES AND CHALLENGES

For Kinship Carers, there are of course two wider families to consider beyond your immediate family and your child's parent(s) and siblings: firstly that of your child - their close friends and other possibly close birth relatives: as well, of course, as your own wider circle of friends and family.

For some children, a real benefit of being in kinship care is that it can help them maintain relationships with parents, siblings and members of their wider family. Your child will have a consistent sense of belonging within their family and friends. However, this can also bring challenges and pressures, as it may well fall on you to organise visits and contact, tell your child about upcoming contact and manage their questions and emotional responses before and afterwards.

Bear in mind that it will be best to start with small steps when introducing your child to your family and friend networks, and approach this in a structured way so your child isn't overwhelmed. Every family structure will be different. However, a suggested order for contact and maintenance of relationships could be:

Birth parents
　　➥ **Wider birth family** ⬎
　　　　　　Your child's friends
　　　　　　　　➥ **Your wider family** ⬎
　　　　　　　　　　Your friends

Thinking contact through

Every contact arrangement with a child's birth parent or family members and experience of contact is unique to each individual, and can also vary over time. A bespoke individual plan and approach is needed, but it will take some time to think about the following points to bring it together. These three questions may be helpful:

- What is the purpose and potential benefit of arranging contact?
- What might be the risks and concerns?
- What needs to be planned/prepared in advance of any family contact?

DIFFERENT TYPES OF CONTACT

- *Unsupervised contact* Your child and their birth parent(s) spend time together on their own
- *Supervised contact* Your child spends time with someone they are not normally living with now, their birth parent or family member, for a period which is supervised by a professional or family member, often at a neutral location such as a contact centre
- *Part of a court order or care plan* The time your child will spend with birth parent(s) when they are not normally resident with them is determined by a court order or care plan
- *Informal and spontaneous* Unplanned time or situations, when your child sees or meets with their birth parent(s) or family members, for example, in the street or at another family member's house
- *Telephone contact*
- *Letterbox contact* A voluntary arrangement to share information about your child confidentially with birth parent(s) or other family members. The letters are monitored and shared with your child when it is agreed that it is appropriate to do so
- *Online contact (e.g. via Zoom)* This is contact through a video platform so your child can see, hear and talk with their birth parent(s) or family member in real time
- *Social media contact* Planned or unplanned

Making decisions about contact

To begin with, a key thing to consider will be the *purpose* of the contact. It could be about maintaining a relationship between your child and their birth parent(s), or for a parent assessment to take place.

Benefits and opportunities

Have a think about the *opportunities* which contact might enable, such as the birth parent(s) reconnecting with the child when they have less day-to-day parenting demands to deal with, which might allow the relationship between them to repair and grow. Contact allows your child to see that their parent is alive and well, which can be very reassuring for them and allows them to keep updated on changes in the lives of their birth parents. It can also provide opportunities for you, their Kinship Carer, to re-connect with your relative ('kin'/the child's birth parent(s)).

There are many other potential benefits of contact: if there is a chance for your child to be reunited with their birth parent(s) at some point then positive, regular contact will increase the chance of this being possible. It can encourage positive family relationships as the child grows up into adulthood, and reduce your child's experience of loss and separation. Contact can improve your child's identity and sense of self, and help them make sense of their past. Your child can gain insight into their birth parent(s) life and they can keep in touch with what is happening in your child's life. Your child may also disclose things to the birth parent(s) or family member during contact and share their views and feelings in a different way than they might with you, their Carer.

Risks and concerns
However, there can be potential risks/concerns around contact, such as

- the behaviour of the parent or the state they are in
- replaying negative aspects of the relationship between the birth parents and your child/children, who may be experiencing unresolved attachment difficulties, or re-enacting them during contact
- contact impacting your child's acceptance of parenting from you as their Kinship Carer [11]

Other concerns may include whether, for example, your child's basic needs are being met (toileting/feeding) during contact, and whether the birth parent(s) will turn up on time or not turn up at all. You may also have concerns about how the birth parent(s) will behave and look, whether they may become angry or upset (dysregulated), or whether they will play with your child in a way which upsets him or her. There may also be concern as to whether they may make your child promises which history suggests they may not keep to, or whether they might share information which is not true or appropriate, particularly about the future or the situation which led to your child not living together with their parent(s). During contact, there can be concerns about a lack of attention being paid to the child, because the parent is using their phone, being distracted or ignoring them.

At the extreme end, behaviour might include some kind of violence, abuse or neglect during contact, or the parent showing possible intoxication, the impact of medication, or be incapacitated in some other way. Naturally, such behaviour, or their parent not looking well, would be troubling, frightening and upsetting for your child, as well as bringing genuine risks. There may also be concern around the parent allowing others to look after your child or abandoning them during contact, or, in rare situations, not returning the child in line with the agreed plan (what is known as a *flight risk*). Sometimes, unfortunately, Kinship Carers have experienced pressure to allow contact when there isn't a contact order in place or pressured to arrange inappropriate amount of contact. Unplanned social media contact may create thorny issues in this respect.

Other impact on your child and you
Finally, it can be stressful to organise and manage contact for your child and their birth parent(s) or family member. It can be a strain practically and/or financially, and it may disrupt your daily routines in the run up to contact, on the day and whilst you are dealing with any fall-out or impact on your child, or yourself.

Your child may become upset around contact, and it may be hard for you to work out what is actually causing that: it could be anxiety about seeing the parent, or confusing feelings, mixed loyalties, disappointment, sadness, worries about you, worries about their parent or themselves. Your child's behaviour may change before or following contact, so it is important that you communicate with school when contact will be taking place so they can understand any changes in behaviour at school and offer support to your child.

Sadly, your child may experience rejection if their parent doesn't turn up, which can have an emotional impact on their self-esteem and self-worth. Equally, seeing their parent well and happy may make them question whether they were '*sent away because they were bad*', if they still don't understand why they are living with you, especially if other siblings have remained with their parent. The contact may be experienced as re-traumatising or confusing, especially if the rules and boundaries during the contact are different than they are used to with you.

Birth parent(s) may also experience feelings of loss and may find it hard to answer questions from their child, such as *'Why did you leave?'* Or *'When can I come home?'* The parents may stay away from contact due to personal circumstances (such as, domestic violence, addiction, lack of transport/finance, difficulties with housing), either because of the difficulties themselves or because they don't want their child to see them struggling.

Contact may also impact you as the Kinship Carer: you may feel anxious in advance, concerned about the fallout for your child: or emotional, distressed or overwhelmed to see the birth parent(s) or the family member (or sad, disappointed and worried if they don't turn up). There may even be conflict between you and the family member, or you and your child, and in the worst circumstances, sadly, you might feel pressured or threatened.

Finding support for contact

If you are related to your child's birth parent, these things can naturally be very upsetting and hard to weigh up, as you consider the options. If you are going for contact, try to plan carefully in advance how to provide or get support afterwards, thinking it all through with your social worker (if you have one) or with a calm, supportive, non-judgmental friend.

There's a lot to think through, and to deal with. Only you know your own particular situation and circumstances, the ups and downs for your child and you, what improves or what gets worse, what the changing positives and negatives are with respect to contact: at times it can seem daunting.

We strongly recommend that you seek support to think through what is in the best interests of your child, and also to seek support for yourself to help you continue to provide that calm, loving, consistent secure base for them as you work out the best way forward. And to look after yourself (*there's more on your own Wellbeing on* p. 50).

CONTACT: KEY POINTS TO REMEMBER

- Make sure everyone involved knows the reason for contact - so there is shared understanding and boundaries
- Each child will need a bespoke plan (in writing) for contact, which considers the relationships and circumstances
- If you are worried about contact or feel it is becoming risky, contact your social worker if you have one. Or, if you feel you need social work support, contact your local authority Children's Services or the charity Kinship, where you can access an online advice finder at Online advice finder - Kinship Compass (p. 66)
- Regularly talk to your child about their feelings about contact
- If you feel changes need to be made to contact arrangements due to lateness/not turning up or the current practicalities making it difficult for those involved, consider changing venues, negotiating changes to timings and so on
- As much as possible, give your child choice of who they see, when they see them and what this will look like, e.g. *what activity, in what setting, for how long etc.*
- As much as possible, maintain a positive relationship between yourself and your child's birth parent(s)
- Maintain a calm approach throughout contact, even if there are strong feelings around with other people
- Do not bring up important issues in front of your child especially if unresolved
- Consider how you, your child and birth parent(s)/family members could be/are being impacted by the contact, and who can help support you all through it
- Let birth parents know about other sources of support you're aware of
- Start a diary to document your child's behaviour before, during and after contact, so that you can work out any patterns, and make provision for any difficulties
- Anticipate that your child may feel quite churned up after contact, and plan for the next couple of days to be peaceful, familiar, nurturing and low-key
- Keep school informed of when contact takes place and any issues that may impact on the support and understanding your child may need in school

In summary

When contact works well, it can increase positive connections and family relations, give your child a deep sense of who they are, and help them to understand and develop acceptance of their situation. So we very much hope that you find your way together to the best outcome for your child, and all involved.

PART 2
Understanding and managing the new relationships

If a child or children are coming to live with you, their family member or family friend, it probably means that they already have a relationship with you. Your relationship, which hopefully has been a happy and warm one up until now, can help your child with settling into and accepting their new home with you. The continuity in relationships, with you, and perhaps with their birth parents and other family members, can positively impact your child's wellbeing and act as a protective factor later in life [1].

However, your child will need to feel that this new arrangement is stable and permanent. They may have worries about the future: what if something happens to you? What if you were to change your mind? Who would look after them then, or where would they live? They may also have worries about what is happening for the parent(s) they are no longer with. Or they may be missing their friends and teachers at a school they can no longer attend, and feeling wobbly. All these concerns, worries and feelings are natural, especially at the beginning or if unexpected things happen further down the line, for example if you were to become unwell.

Even though you know you are doing your best, it's important not to assume your child who has come to live with you feels a sense of stability or permanence, even if they haven't told you they are worried. So, as we mentioned on p. 8, it's important to create a secure home base as soon as possible. Of course it will take a while for your child to really feel that sense of security, but there are some great ways that you, in your role as a Kinship Carer, can help your child with this, over time.

So in Part 2 we'll be looking at what kinds of things will continue to build your secure and trusting relationship with your child: some emotional responses which may be around within your new family structure, and how to manage them, and some ways to support the development of your child's self-awareness and self-esteem. Together, these three things will enable your child to feel secure, loved and able to thrive in your home, school and the wider community. And the most important thing you can do for your child is to help them know, and to feel, *that they belong with you*, as a loved, valued and essential member of your family. Belonging is like the strong root of a plant - it helps your child grow and flourish.

Please remember

Not everything you try will work! Parenting children who have had a hard start to life is not easy. Behaviours that communicate a child's unmet emotional needs may be confusing, difficult to manage or even threatening, and can lead you to sometimes feeling deskilled, frustrated or embarrassed. But you can find ways to return to being calm, open and engaged, and start again. Make sure you have support around you from other adults, to help you do this.

It can be easy to revert back to traditional ways to manage behaviours, which unfortunately don't work for all children, especially those who've experienced trauma. Keep experimenting with the strategies in this book and your Kinship Family App, and find out what works for you and your child (*see* p. 52). The overall aims (and it is a lot to ask!) are to:

Avoid the battle

Maintain your calm, stay present

Manage your own emotions

Treat every day as a new day, and remind yourself that you and your child are both doing your best. Re-read Dr Phil Hammond's advice at the very beginning of this book: perfection isn't the aim, being a good enough Kinship Carer is being a great one!

INTRODUCING THE BELONGING MODEL™

This part of the book follows the Belonging Model™ (King, Perry & Tyler 2024), which identifies the three key components of family care which enable children to feel secure, loved and able to thrive.

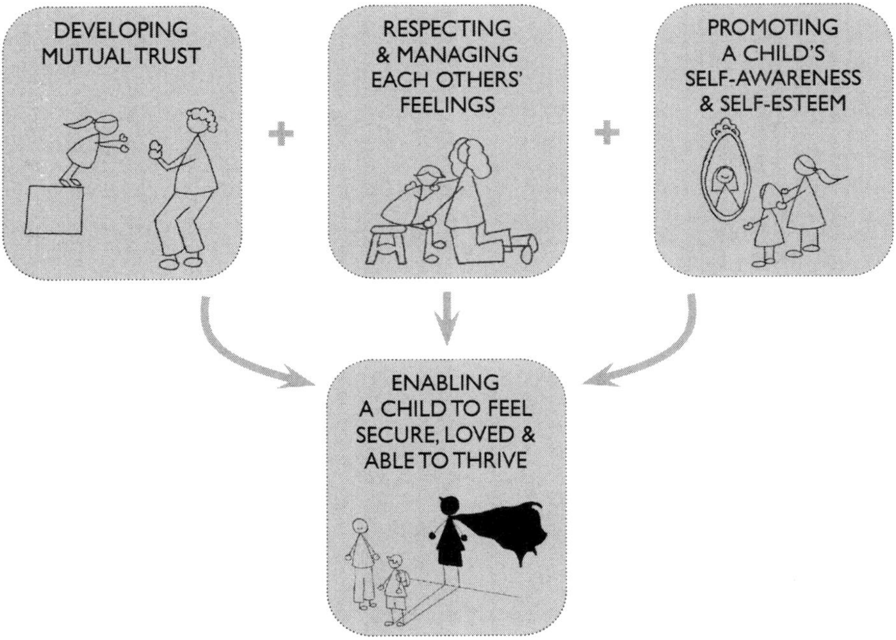

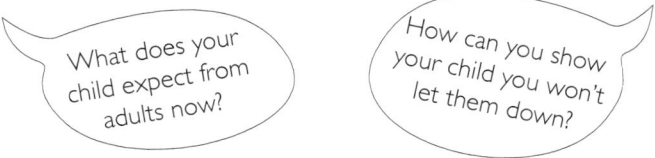

DEVELOPING MUTUAL TRUST   +   RESPECTING & MANAGING EACH OTHERS' FEELINGS   +   PROMOTING A CHILD'S SELF-AWARENESS & SELF-ESTEEM

ENABLING A CHILD TO FEEL SECURE, LOVED & ABLE TO THRIVE

DEVELOPING MUTUAL TRUST

Thinking about trust … what questions are important? These two might give you a starting point:

What does your child expect from adults now?

How can you show your child you won't let them down?

With what you know about your child's history, you can probably understand why it might be hard for them to give their trust to adults now, helping you stay empathic with how they may be feeling.

Being consistent

As in any relationship, a key way to encourage the development of trust is to offer consistency and predictability. For you that might mean, sticking to a daily routine, having a plan for school holidays, maintaining family rituals (e.g. games night on a Friday, bath and wash hair on a Sunday evening), sticking to your word, letting your child know who will be dropping off/picking up from school and having a bedtime routine. Consistency will be different for every family and will be dependent on the age of your child: adolescents will need a sensitive balance of the time they have to enjoy freedom with friends and some agreed times to spend with you and your family, such as sharing an evening meal.

It also means 'being there' for your child, emotionally and physically. You can do this by simply listening first before talking, prioritising connecting with your child before pointing out what they 'should have' or 'could have' done differently: giving them space and time when they need it. Notice their needs and signals, and be curious about their feelings and wishes. Listen to their personal goals (however small!), and say things to help them change their expectation of themselves in a positive direction.

For example, you notice your child really concentrating and appearing to enjoy colouring, but then says '... *they are no good at art*". You could perhaps ask if you can put their artwork on the fridge as you were really impressed with the effort they put in and that it would really brighten up the kitchen. An older child or teenager may feel frustrated with not being able to get into the right frame of mind to tidy their room, but really want it organised: you could perhaps help them break the task down in to a number of smaller tasks, such as, "*Why don't you do the drawers before dinner and after dinner you can have a go at your desk?*" They might not accept your ideas, but their alternative might follow the same principles. Your child may not be used to anyone noticing what interests them, or what they need and like, so start slowly, so they can become used to your attention and hearing positive language about themselves and the feelings they have when that happens.

Togetherness

Children of all ages will benefit from you doing things together with them. Over time, as they enjoy activities with you, their safe, predictable caregiver, your child will begin to associate the positive feelings they have whilst sharing whatever you do together to their relationship with you. So then their day-to-day functioning will improve; they will start to relax and feel, literally, at home. These activities can be anything you both enjoy, but ideally include physical activities and being outdoors, such as nature or sensory walks, dancing, trampolining, cooking, playing board or card games, gardening or planting seeds in a pot for the window ledge, drawing or reading, mending things, dressing up - have fun taking turns choosing what to do together. You can take pictures and make albums together, or write good memories on coloured paper to keep in a memory jar or box to take out sometimes and remind each other of times you've shared.

Importance of play

By having a light-hearted, relaxed and playful attitude, you can help your child to feel connected with you. It can also help reduce their shame when something goes wrong. Show your child with your eyes, eyebrows and smile that you are interested in what they are saying and doing. When possible, make games of the everyday tasks you do together - shopping, tidying, laying the table.

Play is the language of children, and can serve a range of functions for them, as well as being enjoyable. Play has an important part in their learning, working out how to manage feelings, coping with big emotions, building and maintaining relationships, exploring their environment, developing new skills, including their imagination, and confidence, and relaxing. Through play, children can also develop 'cause-and-effect' thinking (*"If I do this, then that will happen"*), as discussed earlier (p. 19), as well as their motor skills (co-ordination and movement, for example) and language skills. Play can also encourage their social and emotional development. Playing is, and needs to be fun, but it's a lot of other things as well.

However, unfortunately, many children who come to kinship care have not had a full range of play experiences. They may play in a way you would expect of a younger child, for example, only playing on their own, or needing to have full control of and attention to their play. Equally for some children, you may notice that their play is limited or repetitive, for example a single action (like lining up their toys on the bed) or play with the same theme (always getting trapped, or etc).

All children should have opportunities for free play, and choice in how they play and what they use in their play. So notice what your child is drawn to and provide plenty of opportunities for them to engage in and develop their chosen play activities - even if this was not what you were expecting, or doesn't seem appropriate for children of their chronological age. Join your child in their play, be alongside them and see if they invite you into their imaginative world.

You can start by noticing and trying some very gentle questioning, for example: *"You look like you're enjoying building with those blocks?"* or *"Does that cat have a name?"* Be careful not to take over! And practise being interested in their ideas, what they come up with. Play can be a valuable way to communicate non-verbally: don't feel you have to talk, just being there physically and engaging through play is sometimes enough. Your child may not have ever experienced an adult following their lead in play, so again, take it slowly and respond to their signals.

Attachment Play

This is a special type of play which encourages the relationship between you and your child to develop. It should be interactive, involve laughter, not need any special equipment and can take place at any time and any place. It can be initiated by your child or by you.

Some examples of attachment play are:

- Piggy back rides
- Playful copycat (mirroring the child's actions - jumping, clapping, facial expression etc.)

- Back drawing - draw a shape or letter on your child's back and they guess what it is! Swap roles between you
- Clapping games - you may remember some from your childhood, or there are lots of videos on YouTube - look up '*Double Double This That*' or '*A Sailor went to Sea*'
- Brushing hair - you brushing your child's and vice versa

Symbolic Play

This is the kind of play where objects represent something else, and can be useful in helping your child process any trauma they have experienced. It's an important milestone in early play development, and therefore important to encourage. So for example, a child might...

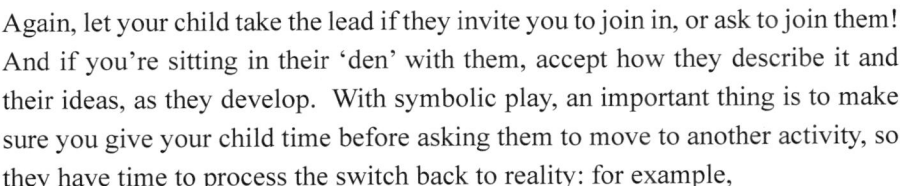

- Use chairs and tables and an old table cloth to make a den
- Turn a box into a spaceship
- Use a block as a phone

Again, let your child take the lead if they invite you to join in, or ask to join them! And if you're sitting in their 'den' with them, accept how they describe it and their ideas, as they develop. With symbolic play, an important thing is to make sure you give your child time before asking them to move to another activity, so they have time to process the switch back to reality: for example,

> *"I've had a lovely time in your den, thank you for inviting me: now I'm going back through the wood to the kitchen to make supper. Could you be back from the den in five minutes, please, when I call you?"*

Importance of language

Your use of language with your child is really important to think about too, in terms of building trust and developing your relationship. You can show empathy through thoughtful and compassionate talk. Your use of language can show your child that you hear them, you empathise, and you want to understand. Some useful sentence starts are:

If your child tells you or shows you through their behaviour how they are feeling, it's important to acknowledge the feeling and what they have shared, even if you can't imagine why they are feeling that way. It can be a big, scary step to let someone else into your emotional world even just a tiny bit, and it may not be something they have done before. So how you reply will influence whether they feel safe to do so, or not, and whether they are likely to feel able to do it again in the future. It will help if you *listen to really understand* their experience, rather than *listening in order to reply*. You could ask someone else to listen to you in these two ways, and feel the difference for yourself! The quality of your attention and body language will convey your genuine interest and care.

And when it's your time to speak, avoid using direct questions such as "*Are you feeling angry?*", because that might be emotionally triggering or confusing if they find it hard to recognise, name and communicate their emotional state. So some useful alternative ways to start your response might be:

"I'm so sorry it's been so hard for you ..."
"I imagine that might have been really painful ..."
"I think you might be letting me know that ...., something like that?"

Try to use a light tone of voice, like you might use when story-telling, rather than a lecturing tone, or even a tense one, if you're feeling rushed. Often it's helpful to talk less, as this can allow you to really listen to your child. Where you can, model the use of emotion language for your child in your own day-to-day language: you can start by referring to yourself in context, for example: "*I feel happy when ...*", "*It made me sad when ...*" "*I felt angry when ...*", and then about your child, for example:

You may not get a response (that is OK!) or you may get corrected (also OK!). It's less about getting it right and much more about showing interest and having a go, rather than making assumptions. Other helpful conversation starters can be found in your Kinship Family App, and in *Conversations that Matter* by Dr Margot Sunderland [2].

RESPECTING AND MANAGING EACH OTHERS' FEELINGS

You and your child will experience lots of different emotions about being together in your new family environment. It's important to accept, and respect that there may well be good underlying reasons for unexpected emotional responses. You can help your child to manage their emotions and we will look at some ways to do this. However, first and foremost, don't forget your own emotions! Which can also be strong and complex, especially when things are new, confusing, or you and your child are tired. Reach out for support and give yourself time to accept these emotions as your new family unit establishes itself, and you get to know each other afresh in your new life together.

It's helpful to deliberately think about what your child may be thinking and feeling (trying to put yourself in their shoes), and what you are feeling about your child. Being curious and paying attention to our children's emotions and behaviours helps us as adults to understand and meet their needs. Showing or modelling your own curiosity helps your child to be more curious about their own experience, and more emotionally aware. Use sentence starters such as:

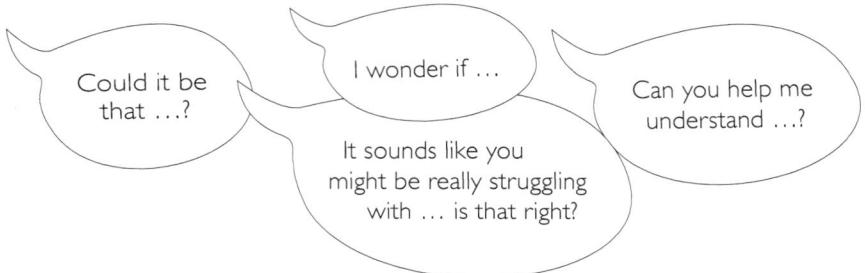

Unconditional acceptance

Unconditionally accepting your child's thoughts, feelings and motives without judgment is not always easy (but really worth practising!). Try to understand and respect your child's feelings without letting yourself judge whether they are different to what you expect: simply listen to what they have to say, even if it's uncomfortable or upsetting to hear. If your child expresses distressing emotions about themselves, for example, *"Nobody loves me"*, *"I'm bad"*, *"You hate me"*, don't challenge them or tell they are wrong: accept and acknowledge what they feel, using curiosity and empathy:

> *"I'm sorry you feel like that, help me understand what might help right now?"*

Our feelings change when we feel accepted, not if we're told we're wrong to feel what we feel! Think about what might be driving your child's behaviours. Your child may well be feeling 'big' emotions which they find overwhelming and don't have the skills to cope with - they may not have had the chance to learn these skills, and need you to help them by being with them until the feelings have been noticed, perhaps shared and spoken about, and then, gradually, pass. Have firm boundaries around behaviour, but accept and respect that the behaviour also has a communication function for feelings for which your child cannot find the words yet, but may well do in time as they come to feel your consistent care and attempts to understand. Your child is so much more than their behaviour, and a boundary isn't a criticism of who they are.

Be aware of your own emotions in response to your child and their behaviours - it will be natural to have mixed feelings at times, and important that you are accepting of this and spend some time reflecting on why this may be. If you do notice that you're not feeling as sensitive or empathic as you usually do, please take this as a sign that you need support yourself, reach out to your support network and focus on looking after your own needs and wellbeing (p. 50).

Supporting your child's emotional literacy development

Emotional literacy is the ability to recognise, understand, manage, and appropriately express our emotions, and includes the understanding we have of ourselves, and how we cope with our feelings and the feelings of others. Disrupted early relationships can negatively impact the development of emotional literacy: your child may not have had opportunity to practise linking their internal feelings with words, or ways to communicate the way they feel.

You can help your child develop their emotional literacy by exploring how emotions 'look' on themselves and others. Play games to show different emotions, like 'copy/guess the expression'. You can also use mirrors in a playful way to explore feeling the physical sensations of making different facial expressions. Identify and name emotions together in books, tv programmes, and movies. Movies such as *Inside Out* [3] can be useful as it introduces emotions as different characters.

It's important that 'learning' emotions is generalised to 'real life', so name emotions when you experience them, for example, *"I'm so happy we are going to the seaside today"*, or *"That surprised me when the cat ran past us on the stairs"*. Encourage your child to do the same. They can start by using non-verbal cues to show their emotions, if they are not ready to verbalise - using a smiley face stamper when they feel happy for example, or squeezing your hand to let you know when they feel scared. Focus on one emotion at a time, starting with the basic emotions that we most frequently see, for example, happy, angry, sad, and scared. Once your child is confident and consistently able to say and show when they are feeling these emotions in context, you can move on to other primary emotions such as fear, interest, surprise, disgust, joy ... little by little, this will give them confidence that all their feelings are acceptable and respected, and can be communicated safely.

Stabilising emotions

A child cannot be expected to bring themselves back into balance after upset without your help ('co-regulation'). So this will mean you working together with your child to introduce and practise strategies to help them manage these big emotions, as a joint effort initially, so they can then start using these more familiar strategies on their own. All our children are different in what works individually for them. So start by creating a 'toolkit' of strategies to explore together at a peaceful and relaxed time. Then try them out and see if they are useful or not, when times are a bit tougher, taking note of what your child seems to respond to and like best.

Here are just a few regulation or calming and balancing strategies you can use together, which your child can then work towards using independently. You'll find many more online.

EMOTIONAL REGULATION

- **Listen to some calming music** which you have chosen at a previously relaxing time together.
- **Do some colouring together** Let your child choose what colours you both use, let them lead and experience a sense of feeling in control.
- **Let them experiment with sensory/fidget toys**
- **Bake together** and then enjoy your tasty creation - share it with others!
- **You could practice a grounding technique** such as the 5-4-3-2-1 technique, where you identify *five* things you can see, *four* you can touch, *three* you can hear, *two* you can smell, and *one* you can taste. You can do this together and then encourage your child to use this when they are finding a situation overwhelming.

PHYSICAL REGULATION

- **Breathing together** Making eye contact and being physically close - so they can feel your presence, you being at their level, not standing over them. Use a calm, low voice and let them see your accepting, relaxed facial expression.

- **Take deep breaths together** Count your breath in through your nose as you count slowly to five, hold your breath for four, and let the breath slowly out through your mouth for a count of seven. Start by doing this for three cycles and then build up in a relaxed way - it's not a competition! The key is to make sure the breath out is longer than the breath in, to really tap into your body's natural relaxation and calming ability. It will get easier the more you practise. There are videos on YouTube which can be helpful to give your child a visual as well, especially if they are young.

- **Also, try to imagine slowly filling your stomach with air when you breathe in** If you put your hand on your stomach when you breathe in you should feel it moving out. You can help your child practise this by lying on your backs together, and putting small soft toys on your tummies and aiming to see if the toys move up when you breathe in, and down when you breathe out. If this ends in giggles, or tumbling teddies enjoying the ride, so be it! Then the activity will have a positive association for your child, and you can have another try again together later.

- **Activity** Kicking balls into a goal, playing catch, skipping, running.

- **Progressive muscle relaxation (PMR)** Tightening and releasing parts of the body, which can help us let go of tension and has a calming effect. You can do this with just your fingers, thumbs and hands, or work through each part of the body, including your face. There are lots of video clips to show you this technique, such as this one youtube.com/watch?v=cDKyRpW-Yuc [4] for younger children: if you google 'PMR scripts' there will be different versions for all ages.

- **Go for a walk outside, spend time in nature** Point out things to each other that you can see, touch, smell and hear, including different kinds of silence or the rhythm of waves and so on. Notice different textures, sensations, shapes … and share them with each other.

CALM BOX

• Something which might help support your child at home is to encourage them to create a **Calm or Self-Soothe box** [5], literally their own small box they can go to help themselves find some calm if they feel anxious, panicky, overwhelmed, or down. The box can contain different items, chosen by the child, things they like, enjoy and find comforting or fun. You can think of the five senses and encourage them to include something for each sense. Each child will have different things, according to their preferences. And they can decorate the box in whatever way they please, to be kept somewhere safe and private, just for them.

Smell	*essential oils, a fragranced soap*
Sight	*a photo of a favourite place or pet*
Sound	*a wind-up music box, or a calming playlist to listen to*
Touch	*a sensory toy, or some soft fabric*
Taste	*a fruity lip balm, or sweet to suck*

• There are further details on the Young Minds website [6], *How to Make a Self-Soothe Box*. As a Kinship Carer dealing with a lot all at once, you could even make one for yourself!

PROMOTING YOUR CHILD'S SELF-AWARENESS AND SELF-ESTEEM
Self-awareness

Self-awareness is your child's ability to monitor their behaviour, respond appropriately to social situations and be aware of their emotions. It's also about them being aware of the things they are good at and not so good at. We all need self-awareness to be able to think back over events, to celebrate, grieve or make decisions about doing things differently in future.

Self-awareness is often underdeveloped in children who have had a disrupted early life, as the brain has prioritised survival and safety over being curious about themselves and being able to notice their responses, skills and so on. We need self-awareness before we can think about building self-esteem, or expecting to be able to manage our emotions (self-regulation) and expand our social skills.

To be able to start developing in these areas a child needs to be calm and alert (regulated) enough to allow their brain to shift their focus from 'survival' to 'exploration' and 'development'. As described on p. 38, co-regulation will be important to enable your child to have the capacity to begin to take the small steps needed for self-awareness, and that will stimulate a positive upward spiral of progress in their social and emotional growth.

Introducing and practising mind-body activities are also helpful for children to better understand and manage their emotions, physical sensations and encourage healthy development, growth and self-awareness.

Body awareness Activities such as yoga, dance or martial arts can improve body awareness and help your child understand the mind-body connection

Mindfulness Can come in different forms such as mindful breathing, eating and walking which can help develop focus and self-awareness. It can help your child monitor and understand their emotions, by focusing on the present moment and their internal experiences. There are lots of books and videos giving ideas of how to introduce this to children, but you can do this simply by going for a nature walk and focusing on the sensory experience (what you can see/hear/smell): doing some mindful colouring together or any craft activity where you use a range of materials and really focus on the task at hand! The breathing technique described in the section on emotional regulation (p. 39) will also be helpful.

Journalling A personal journal where a child or young person can record their thoughts, feelings and experiences, in writing, drawing and other creative media can help them explore their internal world and become more aware of themselves.

You can further help your child to develop their awareness of themselves and theor self-esteem by noticing and encouraging their abilities and strengths, and providing opportunities to use them at home. For example, you could help them make an *All About Me* book together, with photos of them doing things they like and are good at, and if they are willing, this can also be shared with school once they have a secure relationship with a member of staff there who you are confident will take interest in it. You can also use creative activities such as collage, drawing or dance for your child to explore different aspects of themselves. If your child shows an interest in a hobby or activity, consider helping them join a club so they can develop this. And of course there are lots of free ideas and material available on YouTube for any and every activity imaginable.

Self-esteem

Self-esteem, whether positive or negative, is how a child (or an adult) feels and thinks about themselves. If your child believes they are worthy and deserving, then they are more likely to believe they can overcome challenges in life, and reach out for support when they need it. But when a child has had a hard start to life and experienced adversity, and if their development of self-awareness has been impacted, then their self-esteem may also be low or negative. You may notice that your child makes negative comments about themselves, their appearance or things they have done, or feel they'll screw up. Their mood may seem low, perhaps seeming to worry a lot and having anxious thoughts. Self-esteem can be very tied up with our mental health as well, so as adults caring for children, it's something we need to pay attention to.

You can help your child by checking in with them while you are doing an activity together, such as driving to the shops, making dinner. There is a useful guide about how to talk to your child about their mental health at youngminds. org.uk/parent/how-to-talk-to-your-child-about-mental-health [7].

Tell your child you love them and why they are special, highlight their strengths and when they do something well. Your child may not be used to hearing about what they are good at or being complimented, so take it slowly and give short verbal praise and notice their response - it may take some time to get used to the feelings they experience when they hear this. It may be useful to use some of the language introduced earlier in this book, such as "*I wonder if ...*" to explore your child's internal experience (*see* p. 36) and show them you are noticing the early stages of communicating these feelings.

You could decide together on a task your child can do to help around the house, for example. Make sure it's something achievable, something they can do as independently as possible, but is genuinely helpful - you can do it together a couple of times to begin with, and then they could try on their own. If you see they're struggling, encourage them to break the task down into small steps, and maybe do one of the things you know helps them: for example, *"When you went for a walk to the park, it seemed to calm you, do you think that might help now?"*. Encourage your child to do something they are good at or join a school club if there is one, where they can find out about and show their strengths, and learn to enjoy doing so.

You can also model this yourself through positive self-talk, such as *"I feel really proud of myself for getting to Zumba today, even if I could only do half the moves, I got there and I'll go again, I feel great"*. If your child hears your positive language and thoughts, and you giving yourself affirmation for having a go at new things, it will be easier for them to start having a go too. You might find you have fun(!), which you can share with them too.

ENABLING YOUR CHILD'S SENSE OF BELONGING TO DEVELOP

By trying some of the approaches we've been looking at, you will build your child's confidence in developing their abilities, understanding and resilience. They will also be developing their sense of belonging which will enable them to feel secure, loved and able to thrive. Both you and your child will feel the benefits gradually: there is a huge amount to take in, lots of suggestions to think about and things to try; so, take your time and revisit them however often you need to. Little and often is the best way to build a strong foundation for developing the skills, abilities, and qualities that will enable a fulfilled life for you both in your new family structure and in the future.

Family membership

Your child will develop their sense of belonging in your family over time, as you work together on the areas outlined in PART 2. They may have times when they experience a sense of loss of the family members they don't see as frequently, but they will begin to be able to tolerate and manage these difficult feelings through their relationship with you. As their sense of belonging develops, it will allow them to know they are truly loved, valued and respected for who they are, and have an important place in your family. Focus on providing emotional warmth, physical comfort, acceptance and support - and looking after yourself! (p. 50).

Belonging in the wider community

As your child is more settled at home, this sense of belonging will start to extend to their school environment, friendship groups, any clubs they join and the wider community. Many children in kinship care have found it important to have sources of support from outside their kinship family. It's important as far as possible that any networks of support that your child previously found helpful are continued when they move into their kinship care with you. Taking part in school and activities outside their kinship home provide sources of support which can help your child reach their potential and sense of belonging in a wider sense.

In summary: confidence and competence

By developing your relationship with your child and building trust (p. 29) working on recognising, communicating and managing emotions, and encouraging self-awareness and building self-esteem, you will be working together to prepare your child for the challenges of life. Over time, your child's feeling of safety and sense of belonging will grow: at the same time they'll be developing a sense of competence and confidence in themselves. Their ability to take independent action can develop by you allowing negotiation, within firm boundaries, and offering them choice wherever possible. Foster a sense of 'moving forwards together' towards achievable goals: this may be the first time they have 'co-operated' with a parent figure, so take it slowly and calmly.

Finally, now and then, make time to reflect on the journey you are on together, and the progress you are both making. And celebrate it! You both really deserve to.

PART 3
Support services and how
to access them

FINANCIAL SUPPORT

The financial support available to you, the Kinship Carer, will vary from local authority to local authority and is dependent on your arrangement and circumstances. The charity Kinship (kinship.org.uk) has an advice line where you can talk to someone who knows about the benefits on offer, and can support you (0300 1237015). The Family Rights Group has a very useful website specifically on this (frg.org.uk/get-help-and-advice/who/kinship-carers), an advice line 0808 8010366, webchat and forums. You can visit the government website (gov.uk/looking-after-someone-elses-child) which gives more information about the different support on offer. Some of the kinds of financial support you may be able to access are listed below (as of Autumn 2024).

Child benefit	You can apply for this as a parent would gov.uk/child-benefit
Universal Credit	This is means tested, and intended for low income families
Pension Credit	If you are over State Pension age, you can apply for this *in addition to* your State Pension to help with daily living costs, including looking after a child as a Kinship Carer
Guardians Allowance	If both your child's parents have died, you can get this in addition to Child Benefit. Within certain restrictions, you may also be able to access this allowance if one parent has died

If your child is classed as a 'child in need' (p. 5) there may be additional one-off or regular payments you can get: contact your local Children's Services to enquire.

Finally, there are a range of finance support options when a child is being looked after under a Special Guardianship Order (SGO) including the Adoption and Special Guardianship Support Fund (ASGSF) (*see below*). One of the recommendations in the 2024 Kinship report *Breaking Point: Kinship Care in Crisis* [1], is that all Kinship Families should have access to a bespoke version of the ASGSF for appropriate emotional and therapeutic support: so the hope is that this will be a reality in the future.

The Special Guardianship Order (SGO): the requirements of a successful application
What is an SGO?

An SGO is an agreement for a child to live with a 'Special Guardian' until they are 18 years old under The Children Act (1989). It is different to adoption, as it's not a lifelong order, and doesn't legally end the child's relationship with their birth family. An SGO places a child with a guardian permanently, and they will have enhanced parental responsibility for the child. It is usually (but not always) the case that a link to direct family is maintained: however, the SGO does not specifically require this. The child may well have lived with you for some time before the SGO is in place.

A Special Guardian is often, but not always, a grandparent, sibling or other family member: they have to have a close relationship with the child. They can also be a family friend or former foster carer. Children who remain with family members through an SGO have been found to have better behavioural outcomes and mental health as a result of the stability of the placement [2]. SGOs have also been found to support a child to maintain their identity through family and community ties. A high proportion of children under an SGO will have experienced high levels of Adverse Childhood Experiences (ACEs) and some would have been in the care system. If the child has been in the care system, there may be additional resources carers can access.

There is limited research into the experience of those involved in SGOs, and this is an area we need to find out more about: especially listening to the voice of the child and the voice of the Special Guardians [3].

How to apply

If the child is currently looked after, the local authority will need three months' notice of your wish to apply for an SGO. A Social Worker will carry out an assessment of your suitability to become the child's Special Guardian, and then, if approved, you can make an application to your local Family Court. The Court will request the local authority to write a report about suitability, which will look at the background and information of the applicants, the wishes of the child and the birth parents or those with parental responsibility. The court will make a decision whether you can be a Special Guardian. Full details of how to do this are at *CB4 Special guardianship - A guide for family court users* (publishing. service.gov.uk) [4].

What you can decide

Under an SGO you will have joint parental responsibility with the birth parents, but do not have to ask or consult birth parents on decisions you make in relation to bringing up the child, including:

- Where the child lives
- Where they go to school
- Medical treatment they receive

What you cannot do

There are a few things you cannot do as an SGO, without written consent from your child's birth parents:

- Change the name of the child
- Adopt the child, or put the child up for adoption
- Leave the country with the child for a period longer than 3 months
- Decide on medical procedures not related to health - for example, cosmetic surgery, circumcision, and so on.

What is a Child Arrangement Order (CAO)?

A CAO, which used to be referred to as a Residence Order, outlines who a child lives with and spends time with (contact). Parental responsibility is shared between parents and carer, so there is no priority in who makes the decisions. SGOs and CAOs are similar - the main difference is in the *level of parental responsibility*, which is greater with an SGO. We focus on SGOs here, rather than CAO since an SGO gives you, the Kinship Carer, a higher level of parental responsibility and decision-making ability for your child and offers a stronger degree of permanence for the child.

As with an SGO, financial support may be given by the local authority if, following assessment, it is felt this is necessary to look after the child. Support is means tested, discretionary and if payments are agreed, they should be in line with payments a foster carer would get.

Financial Support when under an SGO

There are a range of finance support options when a child is being looked after under a Special Guardianship Order:

- A Special Guardianship Allowance may be given: however, this is means tested. A Social Worker will assess your financial and personal circumstances and notify you if you can access this allowance - this will be reviewed each year. If you can access the allowance, it is based on minimum foster carer allowance figures.
- Support from your local Children's Services must be offered, and this needs to include financial support. Again, this will be subject to an assessment by a social worker. If you do get financial support from Children's Services, it can be a one-off payment for things like bedroom furniture, or if a family is on a low income there is a possibility to get regular payments to support you in your care of your child.
- Children's Services are not to be seen as separate from mainstream services. Children and families with an SGO should be made aware of their entitlement to benefits such as Universal Credit, Child Benefit and Pension Credit.

Your child's birth parents should contribute to the care of their child if this is financially possible. This will be a private agreement between the parents and carers. If they can't or won't contribute, then you can contact the Child Maintenance Service for advice and support. You will find useful information in the *CB4 Special guardianship - A guide for family court users* [4].

Adoption and Special Guardianship Support Fund (ASGSF)

Your child may need therapeutic support to help them to talk through and come to understand their early life experiences, talk about their feelings and explore their emotional world. Some children with an SGO can access the ASGSF to fund this support until the child is 21 (or 25 if they have a Special Educational Need (SEN) or Education, Health and Care Plan (EHCP)). There are certain criteria which determine whether the child can access the funding, including whether the child was previously in care before the SGO, or if a previous SGO broke down. The funding can also be accessed if your child is under a Child Arrangement Order (CAO) to allow for the assessment of a potential special guardian. The fund can be used to access therapeutic support related to trauma and attachment, for example: creative therapies, family therapy, life story work, or therapeutic short breaks. It can also be used to fund specialist assessment to create a therapy plan.

To check if your child is eligible for the ASGSF, please contact your local Children's Services (gov.uk/find-local-council). You can also approach the Virtual School (*see* p. 55) of your local authority to find out who can provide therapeutic support or carry out a specialist assessment. For more detailed information, visit the Adoption and Special Guardianship Support fund for Kinship Families page at Kinship Compass (p. 66).

Finding out about changes to Government policy

The amount and nature of financial and social support will change according to Government policy from time to time. So we also recommend you consult your Kinship Family App, free with this book (*see* p. 52). It's a web App, which means it will be regularly updated free of charge whenever there is a change in Government policy, or new initiatives occur which could help Kinship Carers.

WELLBEING SUPPORT

Looking after your own health and wellbeing

The potential challenges that kinship care can bring may impact your mental health, physical health and wellbeing. It is common to prioritise what your child needs, and forget about making sure you have what *you* need. This can lead to you not being in the best state to cope with the ordinary stresses and challenges which daily life can bring, even aside from your child coming to live with you. So it's important that you find opportunities to look after yourself, so that you can do your best in your new kinship role. Sometimes this may feel almost impossible, but it's not a luxury: it's essential.

> *"I'll be alright if the kids are alright"*
>
> Kinship Carer, Children's Health Scotland

We need to flip this on its head. Being mindful of your own needs will mean you can support others. None of us can be as responsive as we'd like to be to the needs of our children if we are overwhelmed with too much stress. That's why we put the quote from Dr Phil Hammond at the front of the book - your own wellbeing is as important as that of your child.

This means making sure your basic needs are met as far as possible. Often that means the simple things, like trying to get enough sleep, eating as healthily as budgets allow, getting regular exercise and finding ways to do things that you enjoy and find relaxing.

Little changes can make all the difference - walking to school instead of driving, getting fresh air and a stretch, taking the dog for a short walk, taking 10 minutes to kick a football in a nearby park and so on. It's also important that you maintain your relationships with supportive friends, continue going to out to events etc, and regularly speak with people you love to help you keep optimistic about the future. These things may not always be as easy as they once were before becoming a Kinship Carer; but being creative, and making the most of even small moments will help you prioritise pockets of time for looking after yourself.

5 WAYS TO WELLBEING

The NHS suggests a **5 Ways to Wellbeing** approach to improve mental and physical health and wellbeing [5]. You've probably got ways to maintain healthy and positive wellbeing, so here are the so called **5 Ways** to consider with your new family set-up, to see if there's any other area you'd like to focus on a bit more.

- ☏ **CONNECT** in person when possible, or a quick phone call to a family member, staying in contact with your social network, connecting with others with similar experiences. In other words, maintaining (and enjoying) your relationships.
- ⋎ **BE ACTIVE** small pockets of activity in your day, physical movement you enjoy - dance to a favourite song in the kitchen, try a joint activity with your child or a friend, a free fitness programme such as **Couch to 5K** or an online five minute workout. It all helps.
- ◉ **TAKE NOTICE** checking in with yourself and the world around you, being mindful, paying a to present moment - your sensations, thoughts, feelings. You might like to try limiting devices at dinner time, so you can all focus on being there together enjoying your meal. Or try a short mindful walk, noticing what you can see, hear, touch or smell … it could be a joint activity with your child but make sure you're looking after you at the same time, not solely focussed on them. Also try Apps like Smiling Mind App [6].
  - ○ **Conscious breathing** (there are many videos online of ways to do this [7].
  - ☻ **Mindfulness** (see also p. 41) can also help some people improve physical health, sleep and mental health and there is a video specially for Kinship Families [8].
- ▟ **KEEP LEARNING** stay open to new experiences and opportunities: explore YouTube tutorials to develop a skill or figure out how to do things. Try doing something that really interests you: it will boost your self-confidence and self-esteem, and help you build a sense of purpose outside your life as a Kinship Carer.
- ♥ **GIVE** As a Kinship Carer you are already 'giving' full time, to a precious growing person. Check in with family and friends to see how they are doing, and give them the gift of enjoying giving to you, by accepting help from them from time to time! Acts of kindness can give us a feeling of self-worth, positivity, and a sense of reward, so don't forget to notice all the ways you're giving to others at home.

Support groups

It can be so valuable to speak and connect up with others who have similar experiences to you, sharing the positives and the challenges of being a Kinship Carer. You can find out about Kinship Support Groups in your area at compass.kinship. org.uk/groups. These groups will enable you to meet with other Kinship Families, share experiences and exchange advice. If there isn't a Kinship Support Group in your area, you can ask your local authority to set one up through your social worker or contact the Kinship advice phone line (*see* p. 66). There is also a Kinship Together Podcast available on Spotify or Apple Podcasts, which covers a range of issues related to kinship care based on real life experience, stories and advice.

Employment

If you are employed or looking for a job, the Kinship charity have developed a framework which employers can sign up to so they are recognised as a Kinship Friendly Employer [9]. To be recognised, they will need to use Kinship's resources and introduce Kinship Family friendly policies. Look out for employers which have signed up to this, or why not suggest this to your own employer? Ideally all companies would be Kinship Friendly Employers, to ensure that the needs of Kinship Carers are properly recognised and supported in the working world.

MAKING THE MOST OF YOUR KINSHIP FAMILY APP

With this book, you get access to the Kinship Family App. It's a web App, so you can access it on any device via the internet (not through the App store). The Kinship Family App was created for Kinship Families, building on previous work for parents and carers of fostered and adopted children. It aims to support you to understand your child's behaviours, especially if they are challenging, and possibly driven by unrecognised relational and learning needs. This will help you to think about how to help them feel safe and to identify ways to meet those needs together. The App draws on Worth Publishing's books, which have a unique reputation for providing practical guidance to help adults support children and young people who have experienced trauma and loss. The support the App provides is underpinned by what's known as *practice-based evidence*, in other words, the ways parents and educators have found to best support vulnerable children at home and at school. It's compatible with the support provided by social workers and educators (p. 64). When changes in Government policy affect kinship care families, the App's Notes are updated.

When you open the App you'll see a grid of 36 behaviours, which many of us caring for children find challenging to manage and understand. Click on a behaviour which you notice your child often doing, to find out about what might be going on for them and what their behaviour might be communicating. There's a wide range of practical ideas (hundreds!) and suggestions of things for you to think about and try, relating to that behaviour and the needs possibly driving it, to help your child develop, thrive and feel loved and secure.

So, over time, your child will be better able to communicate with you directly, about their needs, feelings, thoughts, worries, hopes and so on, rather than showing you what's happening for them through the kinds of behaviour which can create difficulties for them and others.

KINSHIP	THE KINSHIP FAMILY APP		
Highly anxious	Argues about rules or can't follow	Overly dependent	Rubbishes or rips up what they do
Tends to be a perfectionist	Sulks if not picked/ given special attantion	Resists/avoids tasks/ homework	Rubbishes/rejects what you say/do/offer
Can't sit still	Doesn't want adults physically close	Appears arrogant, omnipotent & controlling	Wants to do things on their own
Resists adult's guidance	Resists difficult conversations	Runs out of house/ class	Misinterprets others' behaviour/comments
Appears manipulative	Hates & rejects praise	Causes hurt to people or animals	Finds transitions & endings difficult
Needs constant reassurance	Reluctant to talk about feelings	Easily distracted	Appears indifferent or uncaring
Rapid mood changes	Talks about feelings a lot & catastrophises	Lies & fabricates	Angry & aggressive
Overuse of internet/ social media	Gets upset easily	Avoids eye contact	Hypervigilant
Clingy	Risky behaviour	Limited imagination	Attention seeking

THE BENEFITS OF USING THE KINSHIP FAMILY APP INCLUDE

- Enabling you to develop a deeper understanding of what needs may be driving your child's behaviour
- Increasing your confidence to care for your child, thinking about relationships and the impact of trauma
- Developing and enriching your relationship with your child, as they increasingly feel not only that you care about and value them, but also that you are beginning to understand, respect and respond to their emotional world
- Helping your child feel safe, settled and able to take part in family life
- Helping your child cope with the challenges and transitions of school life
- Encouraging positive Home-School communication
- Helping you create a peaceful and calm home environment, which everyone can enjoy
- Ways to get the support you may need, and how to access it
- Keep up to date with government policy changes affecting Kinship Families

BUILDING A SUCCESSFUL RELATIONSHIP WITH YOUR CHILD'S SCHOOL

Being in kinship care can help a child reach their potential, as you can encourage and support your child to participate in school and other activities. However, attending and taking part in daily school life comes with its challenges, especially when a child has experienced trauma and loss. Sadly, the experiences your child has already had may impact their school life, their ability to settle to learn and puts a greater emphasis on the need for continuity in their school environment, especially in relationships with supportive adults. If your child's kinship care has meant they have had to move schools, there may be added challenges to their sense of belonging and their own social support network. Or, it may be that your child can remain in the same school, in which case the relationship between you as their Kinship Family and school will need to be established.

The key will be *communication between home and school*, especially during the transition period, but also throughout your child's educational journey. Then, if there are any issues or concerns about or for your nursery or school age child, you can raise them with the school in the first instance, as well as sharing them with your social worker if you have one, so it can be discussed in review meetings and so on, with the school itself.

Our Kinship Family App has a section on ideas to share with school. So it can support your communication with staff and enable you and them to develop a shared understanding of your child's needs together, so you can both provide your child with the most appropriate support. In some cases, the school may also have the Reach2Teach Behaviour Intervention Guide (BIG) App (*see* p. 64) which has compatible content to your App, which would be very helpful. The most important thing is that school staff create a safe, stable and predictable environment in school for your child, so that they have a secure base in school as well as at home with you.

Key roles in school and education: who's who?

There are a range of adults in school settings who may be involved in supporting your child currently or previously. It will be important for you as their Kinship Carer to know who these people are, their role and their responsibilities in relation to your child. In schools, some of these roles are often referred to in their abbreviated form, and there may be an assumption that all carers will be familiar with what people with those job titles actually do! However, if you've never heard of them before, how can you be expected to know? Always feel free to ask: others may not know either. But for ease, here are some of these roles, abbreviations and common responsibilities.

Virtual school (VS)

A Virtual School (VS) is not a physical space with classrooms, but is a function of the local authority: each authority has a VS. The VS aims to support all the children in the care of the local authority through their educational journey. The VS team has a duty to ensure that every child in their remit is fully supported, promoting the best outcomes for each child. The VS team tries to make sure the children and young people in care have the best chance, through the team's advice to and collaboration with the schools which the children and young people attend, and with social workers where necessary.

VS have a responsibility for:

- Children currently living in the care of the local authority (you can check which authority your child comes under) gov.uk/find-local-council
- Children previously in care (including if they moved to an SGO or CAO, or were adopted outside England or Wales)
- Children with a social worker
- Starting between September 2024 and March 2025, the role of the VS has been expanded to include all children in kinship care regardless of legal order - which is great news!

Every VS will have a VS Headteacher (VSH) who will hold overall responsibility. Their role includes championing and promoting educational attendance, attainment and progress of each child, and providing advice and information. This includes children in kinship care (at the time of writing, Autumn 2024). The VS will have links with a wide range of services to support the children they hold responsibility for. The VS team works with schools, especially with the Designated Teacher (DT) (p. 58) which each school will or should have, including discussion around funding to ensure it is being spent in the best way to support your particular child.

Key Adult (KA)

The Key Adult role is not a statutory role, so schools do not have to appoint a member of staff to be this person for your child. However, it is definitely good practice and highly recommended, since knowing who 'their person' is in school may help begin to create that all important feeling of safety your child will need. Schools are well-positioned to offer children in kinship care responsive interactions with caring adults, and providing a Key Adult, who may help mitigate the child or young person's experiences of traumatic and difficult relationships, and be your child's main 'go to' person and point of contact in school, is a really effective way to do this.

The person in the Key Adult role should be a main point of regular contact between you and school (along with other school staff including the Designated Teacher who holds the overall responsibility for your child in school [10]), as well as the 'go to' person for your child when they are in school. Your communication with the Key Adult will be very important throughout your child's time in education, but especially during transitions.

The Key Adult should get to know your child well. This may mean you sharing with them some of your child's early life experiences and details of the current situation at home. It will be useful to meet the Key Adult early on, so you can get to know each other and encourage positive communication going forwards. The Key Adult will also need to access specialist attachment aware and trauma informed training so they can support your child in an informed way, and also be an advocate for your child in the school environment, based on their needs and early experiences. The DT and SENCO (*see below*) will be the appropriate points of contact to discuss relevant training based on the needs of your child.

> Ask school to share with you who the Key Adult will be for your child
>
> Make sure you know how to contact your child's Key Adult via phone and email (if you use email to communicate)
>
> Ask when/where regular meetings will take place

Louise Bombèr (2007) described the Key Adult role in her book *Inside I'm Hurting* [11]. You can tell school about this book if they are not already familiar with this role, or your child hasn't yet been allocated a KA. The book will be an invaluable source for school staff in supporting and understanding your child's needs in a school environment, as will your Kinship Family App (*see* p. 52).

Designated Teacher (DT)

Every school should have a Designated Teacher (DT) who is responsible for supporting children in care, or previously in care, through their education, liaising with the Virtual School, and ensuring that school staff have attachment awareness and trauma informed training. The DT will have the same responsibility for children in a formal kinship care arrangement (one which has been through a court process, *see* p. 3). This is not always the case for informal kinship care arrangements. However, if your kinship arrangement *is* informal, it's always worth meeting with the DT in your child's school, to confirm the set up and responsibility in that specific school and consider together whether there is anything they can do to support your child.

The DT will often be a member of the senior leadership team (SLT) of the school staff, with appropriate experience. They will liaise with the Virtual School team, and, importantly, they should also be your main point of contact in school. Every school is set up differently and it may be that day-to-day communication is with your child's Key Adult or class teacher. It will be important for you to clarify the best person to communicate with (who knows your child best in school) on a day-to-day basis and how you can easily contact them (phone/email or at drop-off or pick-up, if in primary school) on different issues. Please remember that the responsibility for your child is held by the DT if your kinship care arrangement is *formally* arranged and is outlined in statutory guidance issued by the government [12].

In secondary schools, the DT will be less likely to know your child well, purely due to the numbers of children and young people being far greater in a secondary than a primary environment. So although they will hold the same responsibility, it may well be that other staff members will be your daily 'go to' people. Every school set up will be unique and a 'Team Pupil' approach (*see* p. 62) will ensure the key staff in school are all kept informed of daily updates, and you know who your best point of contact will be for what.

It's really important that you know who you can turn to. It may be that the school is used to working with kinship care families, in which case, you may find they have some very familiar set-ups and processes that have been shown to work for other families and which can be tailored for you and your child. However, if you're the first Kinship Carer the school has had, remember that the pathways and practices you help them develop will really help those who come after you.

Most children in kinship care will not be considered as looked after by the local authority. However, there will be some children who are, perhaps if they were in foster care before coming to live with you. If your child is classed as looked after then they will have a Personal Education Plan (PEP). This is a statutory plan which outlines their educational progress to date and plans for going forward; it is part of their overall care plan. The PEP will be started by a social worker and then the DT will develop and review the plan with relevant staff in school. The plan should reflect your child's current educational needs, and it will detail what should happen so they can fulfil their potential. The PEP will be regularly reviewed as part of the statutory review of the looked after child's care plan.

As it is only children classed as looked after by the local authority who will have a PEP, a social worker will always be involved in this process. Most children in kinship care will not have a PEP, and the support they receive in school will be based on their presenting need.

Special Educational Needs Co-Ordinator (SENCO)

This person holds responsibility for children with a Special Educational Need (SEN). If your child does have a SEN or you think they do, this will be the person to talk to about the support they will need in school. Remember there are four areas of SEN, and a child's needs can fall in more than one area:

- Cognition and learning
- Social, emotional and mental health
- Communication and interaction
- Physical and sensory

If your child's needs are complex, the SENCO may suggest an application for an Education, Health and Care Plan (EHCP) to get funding to provide the support they need in school. This will involve an assessment carried out by the local authority. You can watch a webinar on what this will involve at coursewedo.com/building-effective-ehcps-webinar-with-consultant-educational-psychologist-dr-rachael-king

Emotional Literacy Support Assistant (ELSA)

ELSA's are school staff (usually Teaching Assistants) who are trained and supervised by Educational Psychologists to develop and deliver programmes of support to meet the emotional needs of children in schools through individual or small group work. The ELSA training is based on the understanding that when children's emotional needs are met in school they will learn better and be more content in the school environment. The ELSA title can only be used if the staff member is accessing regular, ongoing supervision from an Educational Psychologist. They help support a wide range of needs including loss and bereavement, self-esteem, relationship difficulties, managing strong feelings and emotional literacy. You can ask your school if they have an ELSA and if your child can be supported by them in school.

Educational Psychologist (EP)

Educational Psychologists can play an important part in supporting children in Kinship Care. Each local authority offer will differ and you can find out about your area by visiting the Local Offer page of your authority's website. You can also talk to your school SENCO about the local EP service. EP's also work outside their authority and can offer a range of support options for working with children with SEN, carrying out needs assessments, working therapeutically, in multi-professional teams and supporting families. When the work is outside of the authority it will need to be funded independently: this could be by yourself, or, you can talk to the Virtual School in your local virtual school to see if there are any funding options through them, as these can vary between authorities. Some Virtual Schools have an EP who works as part of their team.

DEVELOPING A SENSE OF BELONGING IN SCHOOL

Belonging is so important for your child, both at home and at school, and can't be taken for granted. So there will be some important considerations to work through with school early on so that there is agreement and a shared understanding between you and the staff as the foundation. This can include:

- **Confidentiality** The need to ensure that personal information you talk about with school will only be shared when appropriate with those in 'Team Pupil' (*see below*), and shared with relevant new staff, so you don't need to keep repeating it
- **Legal arrangement** Where there is a legal arrangement, it is important that the school knows what the current arrangement is, what that means for the school, for contact arrangements, and who will make key decisions.
- **Child protection and contact** Individual restrictions on birth parents or family members in relation to contact due to a legal order, if a protection plan is in place. Let the school know and ensure the staff have a robust safeguarding plan in place to manage any situations which may arise.
- **Social and emotional needs** Behavioural patterns, triggers, calmers, transitional objects they may wish to bring into school (p. 10): any attachment needs and trauma history.
- **Explanation for peers** If you have agreed a 'story' or narrative your child will use when talking to friends in school about their situation, then share this with school.

It may also be useful for you to:

- Arrange a meeting with the **form tutor (secondary) or class teacher (primary)** before the start of the school year to update them on your child's strengths and needs, personality, current situation, upcoming events, social and emotional needs (see above).
- Identify who the **Mental Health champion** in school is, and what support they offer.

- Ask if the school has an **ELSA** (Emotional Literacy Support Assistant) and what support they can offer.
- Ask if school is using the **Reach2Teach BIG App** [13] or **Action for Inclusion Tool (AFIT)** [14], as these are compatible with your Kinship Family App.
- Talk to school about the concept of **'Team Pupil'**, in other words, identifying a small tight team of staff who will be there for and looking out for your child. Identify together who could be in this team and how responsibilities will be shared amongst the staff [15]: who your key contact person is, and your child's.
- Ask if the school use a **Pupil Passport/One Page Profiles:** this is a summary page shared with school staff which will outline your child's strengths and needs in their learning, and school setting, any triggers and calmers and their key Team in school. If school do use these, ensure it is co-produced/written with yourselves, key school staff and your child [16].
- Ask school if they have anything in place to encourage **peer-to-peer support** of children in kinship care.

WORKING WITH SCHOOL TO ESTABLISH A SECURE LEARNING PLATFORM FOR YOUR CHILD

As we've already discussed, a hard start to life and experiencing adverse events can impact a child or young person's ability to communicate, concentrate and focus, and also have an adverse effect on their confidence and peer relationships. The priority must always be for your child to develop a sense of feeling safe in the school environment, what we again might call *felt safety*. This will need to be established through a trusting relationship, with their Key Adult, and ideally with class and subject teachers. Your child will also need to have safe spaces within the school grounds, established plans for when they become really upset or agitated or anxious, and a consideration of any sensory needs and accommodations for these. It will be important for the school to monitor friendships and any possibilities of bullying.

All staff in school will need to understand what it may look like if your child is struggling or feeling overwhelmed and what to do/say and not to do/say at those times to best support them. This will be different for every child and should be communicated through the Pupil Passport system (*see above*) with your child's Key Adult being the advocate for them. Only when their feeling of safety has been established can we expect your child to begin to settle to engage in their learning tasks and make friends, so all the adults involved will need to be patient! None of us build a sense of safety overnight, if things have been challenging for us.

Schools will have differing levels of attachment aware and trauma informed training, which will impact the staff's level of understanding of your situation and your child's needs. Ideally each school would have a 'Relational Policy' rather than a 'Behaviour Policy', and a focus on being curious about behaviours which may be communicating unmet emotional needs (again, they can use the Reach2Teach BIG App to learn more about this, (p. 64)).

However, regrettably, the reality is that the majority of schools continue to use punitive approaches to any behaviours which do not conform to their often overly strict policies and rules, especially at high school/secondary school. Under such systems, the acknowledgement that a reward/punishment approach is often ineffective with children and young people who have experienced a hard start to life, and have unmet emotional needs, is non-negotiable. Behaviours in school which may be classed as 'disruptive', 'defiant' or 'hard to manage' are actually a communication of a child's needs, when they aren't able to tell us about them in any other way.

So a lack of understanding of this amongst school staff or senior management, and no recognition of the need for a relational approach for them, can create problems for your child. This might be especially true if there is an increase in such behaviours at difficult times - such as before/after contact visits. So it can be helpful if Kinship Families share details of contact dates with parents, siblings or other family members with school so the staff can understand and make accommodation around these times. It is also important to share other times which may be challenging but not always obvious to school staff, such as anniversaries, unstructured term endings, special days out, when things are less predictable and your child may feel less in control, or unsafe.

You (and the social worker if you have one) may need to advocate for a different, more relational approach. The Designated Teacher has a legal responsibility to help with this as well (p. 58) so should be a good person to involve.

Working with the school with your Kinship Family App

The approach in this book and the Kinship Family App is underpinned by *practice-based evidence*, tried-and-tested parental and educational experience, as well as research carried out in the UK and US. Your Kinship Family App can be used in partnership with the teachers' educational version, the Reach2Teach BIG App (Behaviour Intervention Guide) and the schools-based Reach2Teach AFIT (the Action for Inclusion Tool). AFIT enables schools to track changes in your child's capacity to settle to learn over time, as they gradually feel safer and more secure in school, as suggested by changes in their behaviour and engagement in positive, supportive relationships and meaningful tasks. The needs analysis and helpful suggestions offered in all these APPs are compatible with the work carried out by social workers. You can therefore rely on these resources to provide a mutual common understanding of what will best support your child.

If your child's school doesn't use these tools at the moment, you could suggest they do so (coursewedo.com), so that together with Team Pupil, you can co-create a joined-up approach, especially if your child has been struggling to learn or feel safe and comfortable in school.

The *impact* of supporting your child through these ideas and strategies can be correlated by AFIT with changes recorded by the Strengths & Difficulties Questionnaire (SDQ), used by social workers as part of their formal assessments, alongside your child's attendance at school. AFIT is the only schools-based software to offer this.

Partnering with school staff and allied professionals in these collaborative ways, and communicating through a shared attachment aware, trauma informed language, will all help build strong relationships between you to better enable your child to thrive. You'll be working together holistically to support your child across home and school, providing them with much needed stability and consistency. The safer your child feels, the more they'll be able to learn, make friends, have fun and fully thrive - which is what we all want!

If it *"takes a village to raise a child"*, then this book and these tools together with the contacts and resources we've mentioned, will provide great ways for the adults in the village - yourself as the Kinship Carer, your wider Kinship family, school staff, social workers and others - to give your child, or children, the support they so richly deserve.

Useful contacts to help and support you

Adoption and special guardianship support fund (ASGSF)
Guidance on how to apply for the fund gov.uk/guidance/adoption-support-fund-asf
Phone: 01223 463517 Email asf@mottmac.com

Bullying UK Information and advice for parents, carers and pupils related to bullying
bullying.co.uk Free helpline 0808 8002222

Buttle UK Emergency funding for vulnerable children in need to attend boarding school
buttleuk.org

Calculate your entitlement to benefit
entitledto.co.uk/benefits-calculator/Intro/Home?cid=5573fa7e-42b2-4482-899c-22b550bbe320

Child Bereavement UK Support for children, young people and families impacted by
bereavement Helpline: helpline@childbereavementuk.org   Phone: 0800 0288840

Civil Legal Advice (CLA) Free and confidential legal advice
gov.uk/civil-legal-advice   Phone: 0345 3454345

Corum Children's Legal Centre Charity offering legal information, advice and
representation to children, young people, their families, carer
childlawadvice.org.uk/information-pages/family-and-friends-care

Family Rights Group Database of local authority Kinship Policies and Contacts per region
frg.org.uk/policy-and-campaigns/kinship-care/local-authority-kinship-policy-and-contacts

First4adoption Further information about the ASGSF
first4adoption.org.uk/adoption-support/financial-support/adoption-support-fund

Parents Protect Help to protect children from online sexual abuse and exploitation
parentsprotect.org

Kinship National charity offering support for all Kinship Carers including an advice line
kinship.org.uk Monday-Friday from 9:30am to 2:00pm Phone: 0300 1237015

Kinship Card Discount card to use with retailers, still in its early stages, but you can sign up
now kinshipcard.co.uk/about-us

Kinship Compass Connect with other kinship carers, get advice and information, access
workshops compass.kinship.org.uk

Kinship friendly employer scheme kinship.org.uk/get-involved/kinship-friendly-employers

Kooth Free safe and anonymous support for young people kooth.com

National Association of Therapeutic Parenting (NAOTP) Further information about Therapeutic Parenting nnaotp.com/what-is-therapeutic-parenting Phone: 01453 519000

NSPCC PANTS Keeping children safe from sexual abuse (for younger children) nspcc.org.uk/keeping-children-safe/support-for-parents/pants-underwear-rule

Recovery Help for drug or alcohol rehabilitation recovery.org.uk Help and advice line: 0203 5530324

Young Minds Mental Health charity offering information and advice for young people, parents and carers youngminds.org.uk Help finder: youngminds.org.uk/parent/find-help Helpline: 0808 8025544

Your local citizens advice office citizensadvice.org.uk

References

INTRODUCTION

1. **Save the Children (2007).** *Kinship Care* (leaflet). Save the Children Fund 2007.

2. **Kinship (2022).** Webpage - Why we exist - Kinship - The kinship care charity [accessed August 2024]

3. **Kinship Care Parliamentary Taskforce (2020).** *First Thought Not Afterthought: Report of the Parliamentary Taskforce on Kinship Care.* Available at: frg.org.uk/involving-families/family-and-friends-carers/cross-party-parliamentarytaskforce-on-kinship-care [accessed: 10 June 2024]

4. **Kinship (2024).** *Breaking Point: Kinship Care in Crisis.* Kinship. Available at: kinship.org. uk/breaking-point/key-findings-support [accessed: 3 July 2024]. This summarises the experiences and views of 1,700 kinship carers in England and Wales from their responses to an annual survey.

PART 1

1. **Peak. L. (2022).** *Why social work needs to become more skilled in kinship care'.* Kinship.

2. **Peak. L (2019).** *State of the Nation Survey 2019.* Grandparents Plus.

3. **Hunt, J. (2012).** *Practising in Kinship Care: The perspectives of social workers.* Kinship and Cardiff University.

4. **National Scientific Council of the Developing Child (2015).** *Supportive Relationships and Active Skill-Building Strengthen the Foundations of Resilience - Working Paper 13.* Center on the Developing Child, Harvard University.

5. **Boyden, J. & Mann, J. (2005).** Children's risk, resilience, and coping in extreme situations (Chapter 1).
In *Handbook for Working with Children and Youth: Pathways to Resilience across Cultures and Contexts.*

6. **Bombèr, L. M. (2017).** *Inside I'm Hurting.* Worth Publishing: Broadway, UK.

7. **National Institute for Health and Care Excellence (NICE) (2021).** *Looked after children and young people.* Public Health England, October 2021.

8. **Life Story Book work for Kinship Carers** kinship.scot/wp-content/uploads/2024/02/Life-Story-book.pdf

9. **Bombèr, L. M. (2017).** *Inside I'm Hurting.* Worth Publishing: Broadway, UK.

10. **Bramlett, M.D., Blumberg, S.J. (2007).** Family structure and children's physical and mental health. *Health Aff (Millwood). 2007 Mar-Apr;26(2):549-58.*

11. **Moyers, S., Farmer, E., & Lipscombe, J. (2006).** Contact with family members and its impact on adolescents and their foster placements. *British Journal of Social Work, 36(4), 541-559.*

PART 2

1. **Vis, S. A., Handegård, B. H., Holtan, A., Fossum, S., & Thørnblad, R. (2016).** Social functioning and mental health among children who have been living in kinship and non-kinship foster care: Results from an 8-year follow-up with a Norwegian sample. *Child & Family Social Work,* 21(4), 557–567

2. **Sunderland, M. (2015).** *Conversations That Matter.* Worth Publishing: Broadway, UK

3. **Docter, P., & Del Carmen, R. (2015). Inside Out.** *Walt Disney Studios Motion Pictures.*

4. **youtube.com/watch?v=cDKyRpW-Yuc** Progressive Muscle Relaxation for children, GoZen [accessed July 2024]

5. **Bombèr, L. M. (2017).** *Inside I'm Hurting* (p. 206). Worth Publishing: Broadway, UK

6. ***How to Make a Self-Soothe Box*** - A blog written by people who have found using their self-sooth box helpful youngminds.org.uk/young-person/blog/how-to-make-a-self-soothe-box [accessed July 2024]

7. **Webpage - youngminds.org.uk/parent/how-to-talk-to-your-child-about-mental-health** How to talk to your child about mental health, Young Minds [accessed July 2024]

PART 3

1. **Kinship (2024).** *Breaking Point: Kinship Care in Crisis.* Kinship. Available at: kinship.org.uk/breaking-point/key-findings-support [accessed: 3 July 2024]

2. **Family Action (nd) Information leaflet:** *How is Special Guardianship Order different from other forms of caring?* Family Action, London, UK.

3. **Ramoutar, L. & Hampton, L. (2024).** Exploring special guardianship: experiences of school belonging from the perspectives of the young people, guardians, and designated teachers. Educational Psychology in Practice. *Published by Informa UK Limited, trading as Taylor & Francis Group. School of Education, University of Exeter, Exeter, England.*

4. **HM Court and Tribunal Service. (2014, April 1st).** Special guardianship: guide for family court users (CB4) d.docs.live.net/5332bd60d370ddd8/1%20Independent%20practice/1%20Independent%20work%202024-20 [accessed July 2024]

5. **Aked. J, Marks. N, Cordon. C, Thompson. S. (2011).** *5 Ways to Wellbeing* New Economics Foundation (NEF)

6. **Smiling Mind App** smilingmind.com.au/smiling-mind-app [accessed July 2024]

7. **Every Mind Matters - Conscious Breathing example** youtube.com/watch?v=wfDTp2GogaQ [accessed July 2024]

8. **Kinship Care - Mindfulness for Kinship families** youtube.com/watch?v=pGlmZGro57k [accessed July 2024]

9. **Kinship - Kinship friendly employer information** kinship.org.uk/get-involved/kinship-friendly-employers [accessed July 2024]

10. **Department for Education (2018).** *The designated teacher for looked after and previously looked after children.* DfE, London.

11. **Bombèr, L. M. (2017).** *Inside I'm Hurting.* Worth Publishing: Broadway, UK

12. **Department for Education (2018).** *The designated teacher for looked after and previously looked after children.* DfE, London.

13. **Reach2Teach Behaviour Intervention Guide (BIG) App,** available at coursewedo.com

14. **Action for Inclusion Tool (AFIT),** available at reach2teach.net

15. **Bomber, L. M. (2016).** *Attachment Aware School Series.* Worth Publishing: Broadway, UK.

16. **Morewood, G. D. (2014).** *Our Effective Alternative to IEPs (Student Passports),* Optimus Publishing, SEN Hub Magazine, p. 10-11

When all you have is breathing

When all you have is breathing
and no-one is behind
it's up to you with feeling
to be the loving kind

When all you have is breathing
and no-one seems to care
it's up to you with feeling
to show them you are there

When all you have is breathing
and no-one seems to know
it's up to you with feeling
to find the way to go

When all you have is breathing
no chorus to this song
it's up to you with feeling
I really do belong

When all you have is breathing
and someone really cares
it's up to you with feeling
to tell them you are theirs.

RT
Previously Looked After Child